THE
FULL FEE
AGENT

CHRIS VOSS AND STEVE SHULL

THE
FULL FEE
AGENT

*How to Stack the Odds in Your Favor
as a Real Estate Professional*

The Full Fee Agent

How to Stack the Odds in Your Favor as a Real Estate Professional

ISBN 978-1-5445-3663-7 *Hardcover*
    978-1-5445-4085-6 *Paperback*
    978-1-5445-3664-4 *Ebook*
    978-1-5445-3665-1 *Audiobook*

"Real estate agents are the greatest bargain on planet earth."

—Chris Voss

We would like to dedicate this book to every

real estate professional who truly wants to excel in this business.

Every day, you go out into the world, working hard to be trustworthy,

competent, and a straight shooter, with little or no appreciation.

Most of your clients undervalue your service and think they can do

your job better than you. It is virtually impossible for any buyer

or seller to fully understand the complexity of your

efforts and the skill and knowledge required.

If they only walked one day in your shoes, perhaps

they would have a very different opinion.

Hopefully this book will give you the insight and wisdom to

conduct your business to the best of your ability, and live with

less stress and greater ease in everything you do.

—Steve Shull

IT IS NOT ABOUT GETTING IT DONE...
IT'S ABOUT DOING IT EVERY DAY.

CONTENTS

FOREWORD

Elaine Stucy

DECEMBER 12, 2000 WAS THE EVENING MY LIFE CHANGED FOREVER. Desperately in need of improvement in my sales results, I contacted Steve Shull, a business coach I had heard on a conference call. He sounded strong, confident, even intimidating. It didn't matter, I urgently needed direction. Did I say direction? Instead, I got an earthquake! Steve initiated a radical about-face in my career and life. In one remarkable—and very short—conversation, the man showed me the blue-sky potential of a career in real estate. I believed him. He changed my direction all right... and transformed my life.

After that conversation, I knew better than to expect anything conventional from Steve's coaching. That was twenty-one years ago, and to this day, he can't let it rest. Steve is still a man on a mission of discovery into how to help real estate brokers become the best of the best and enjoy the process.

In my early years, his coaching was all about discipline, focus, and goals. He relentlessly taught me how to create $1 million a year in revenue. Steve instilled belief—not blind faith, but credibility worth trusting. Whatever he told me to do, I jumped in with both feet, usually with great results. Over the years, I built a boutique brokerage and sold to a major brokerage firm, where I still practice.

When Chris came on board a few years ago, it took things to a whole new level. What we were doing had been working well, but Chris's insight into human behavior was like rocket fuel. Steve went all in, so I did too, and the resulting transformation made my business more successful and sustainable than I ever imagined.

Above all, Steve has uncanny insight and perception. He is always learning, investigating, experimenting, and improving, and he sees to the heart of situations and people in startling ways.

A recurring lament from Steve is that no matter the level of success, or lack thereof, his clients share puzzling maladies. Why such constant stress and drama in agents' lives? Why are agents always operating out of fear? How is it that many are afraid to take a day off (you know who you are), reluctant to tell clients when they are taking a vacation, making everything personal, striving constantly to be liked, cutting fees to get business, worried, attached to every outcome, determined to convince, or too superstitious or fearful to try something different? A small percentage transcend, but most suffer.

Steve always admonished us that there is no magic pill in real estate. On that prescription, he may be proving himself wrong. He and Chris are giving the real estate world a book with all the effects of a magic pill, a great elixir. Oh, it might be hard to swallow for some. It takes courage and spirit to let go of practices that don't work well, to open up and absorb a new way. It takes even more courage and faith to suspend resistance, and believe there is an even better way when what you do is working. Within these pages is the extraordinary wisdom to create a bridge of trust between people, and make the process of a real estate career a wholly beneficial, joyful experience. I hope you have the courage to try.

INTRODUCTION

*How you do business is more important
than how much business you do.*

On a Saturday afternoon in the fall of 2016, everything I thought I knew about selling real estate went out the window.

I was by no means new to the business. Over the previous twenty-five years, I had sold real estate in high volume, grown real estate startups and training companies, and owned a successful real estate brokerage that I helped build from scratch. Most importantly, I had coached the best of the best in the industry for decades, constantly perfecting my methods to help agents take the next step in their business and reach heights they once thought impossible. I studied real estate agents nonstop, and there was probably no one else on the planet earth who understood them better.

After living and breathing real estate for that long, I was convinced I had this thing wired from beginning to end. If you wanted a straightforward blueprint for achieving greatness, I served it up on a platter...or so I thought.

I was wrong. That day, I realized I had to rewrite the playbook from scratch.

It wasn't the first time I found myself taking on a radical life change virtually overnight. I did it when a knee injury cut my professional football career short after just four years with the Miami Dolphins. I did it when I finished my MBA and took a job on Wall Street, and again when I left that job to start my own trading company with a colleague.

The world of finance wasn't my final stop, though. Sometime in 1990, someone gave me a recorded interview of two Long Beach, California real estate agents, Kim and Daryl Rouse. This duo was articulate, energetic, and dynamic. They had a plan, they knew how to execute it, and in just their second year as agents, they were on track to sell one hundred homes. Given that the average agent sells four to six homes per year, that was impressive stuff.

As I listened to the interview, something clicked inside me. Everything they were saying made total sense. It was all repeatable. I could envision myself doing the same thing, and generating the same result.

That was all the spark I needed for another radical change. So in 1991, I packed up all my belongings and headed to Southern California —Fullerton, to be exact. I didn't know anyone or anything about real estate, but the interview with Kim and Daryl just kept playing in my head: contacts equal leads...leads equal appointments...appointments equal listings...listings equal sales!

That progression was going to be my new life. I was a man on a mission, and as usual for me, there was no Plan B—I just assumed I would succeed. (Some say that successful people have a certain delusional quality about them, and I tend to agree.)

I wasn't trying to reinvent the wheel. I attended many seminars and workshops, listened intently to one top agent after another, and did exactly what they were doing. I was motivated, disciplined, and looking for any edge I could get. Because of my sports background, I was no stranger to hard work and didn't struggle with the idea that I needed to prospect three to five hours a day. My goal was to make fifty contacts every day, and that was simply what had to get done.

I could hardly have picked a worse year to start this career. At one point, my partner and I had forty listings and no escrows. If four people walked into an open house, it was a huge success. "Multiple offers" meant buyers were writing offers on multiple properties to see where they could get the best deal. Most listings took somewhere between ninety days and a year to sell—if they sold at all. Times were scary, and it was hard not to second guess my decision to become a real estate agent.

But after knocking on 200 doors a day, five days a week, and calling every expired listing every day, the momentum finally kicked in. By the end of 1991, my first year in real estate, my partner and I had closed fifty-three transactions in one of the most difficult markets ever.

In my second year, I came up with the idea of creating a coaching program for agents. I knew what worked, I had put it into practice, and I believed I could help other people do the same. To my knowledge, at that point, there was no such thing as real estate coaching—plenty of speakers and trainers, but no coaches.

So, I teamed up with one the biggest speakers in the business, and that's how the first real estate coaching program was born. It took off almost immediately. When we first introduced the program to a

Coldwell Banker office in Las Vegas, we signed up nine agents. Then, at a much larger workshop in San Francisco, we signed up ninety more.

The original format was a fifteen-minute phone call every other week for one hundred dollars per month, and agents completed a daily activity report and faxed it to me every week. The fax machine was going nonstop, as were my coaching calls. Soon, my schedule was filled with clients, and we hired nine other full-time coaches.

This was what I was meant to do—not sell real estate myself but help other agents become the best they could be. I'm a coach at heart, and my curiosity and desire to figure out this industry never fades. So, in 1996, I went out on my own and formed Performance Coaching, and I stayed the course for two decades...until that day in the fall of 2016.

That was the day I started reading a book a coaching client had given to me: *Never Split the Difference* by Chris Voss (the coauthor of this book). In that bestseller, Chris shared the negotiation strategies he had learned over two decades as a hostage negotiator for the FBI. When the book came out in 2016, it completely upended the prevailing wisdom on negotiation, calling into question the logic-driven, yes-focused methods everyone took for granted. Since then, it has become the go-to guide for business negotiators everywhere, and Chris is one of the most sought-after negotiation trainers in the world.

The title was what drew me in. Never split the difference? In real estate deals, agents almost *always* ended up splitting the difference! If that was a flawed strategy, I had to find out why. Just like the 1990 interview with the two Long Beach agents, Chris's book turned out to be a life changer.

Up to that point, I had viewed real estate as a linear process, just as

I had been taught from the beginning. Nuts and bolts 101. Looking at the business through the lens of fact, logic, and reason, everything could be synthesized into a foolproof series of clearly defined actions. There was no emotional component to my calculations because emotions just got in the way of rationality.

Big mistake.

Thanks to Chris, I finally saw what I had been overlooking: **you can't overcome emotion with fact, logic, and reason.**

Chris's message hit me like a lightning bolt. The approach I had been using for my entire career was completely backwards. I had been trying to eliminate the volatile emotions inherent in the real estate business, but that's impossible—it's simply against human nature. *You can't overcome emotion with fact, logic, and reason.*

FOMO AND THE TEMPTATION OF MORE

In short, I had gotten really good at doing the wrong thing. It worked—my clients got great results...but only by repeatedly conquering a problem they could have been avoiding altogether.

I call that problem the agent's doom loop: chase, convince, and close.

Virtually every agent lives in this cycle. It's not what you signed up for—if you're like most agents, you got into this industry to earn a six-figure income, be your own boss, and have flexibility in your schedule. But in reality, that six-figure income is elusive, being your own boss is harder than you ever imagined, and "flexibility" really means being on call 24/7.

Why? Because of fear.

That's the real driving force in the residential real estate industry. To be more precise, it's the fear of missing out (a.k.a. FOMO). Why else do you work the way you work? You don't chase on a daily basis for the thrill of it. You don't convince because you love twisting arms. You don't take every opportunity to close because you think people love being pressured.

You do all this because you fear what will happen if you don't. As human beings, we've been conditioned to believe that our inside world is directly related to the outside world. As a result, we spend our entire lives trying to get the outside world to line up in a way that makes us feel good on the inside. If we can achieve certain external results, we'll finally be happy.

That's a nice story, but it's simply not true. In reality, the inside and outside world operate independently from each other. The world will go on the way it does regardless of how you feel about it, and no external results will ever bring the lasting joy and inner peace you crave in your life.

This isn't just idle philosophy—the doom loop is a direct byproduct of this false way of thinking. You're a commissioned salesperson. You only get paid when you close a sale. The prospect of not getting that result sends your mind to all the dark places. Unconsciously, you think that your business will fail...you'll go broke...you'll starve...you'll *die*. This may sound like a gross exaggeration, but for most real estate agents, this is their life. No money equals death.

This way of thinking and feeling puts you in full-on survival mode. You chase, convince, and close as if your life depends on it because in your mind, it actually does. But the more you follow this doom loop, the more you push people away, which then fuels more feelings around lack and limitation. It's a never-ending cycle of doom and gloom.

So, with a market that's overflowing with licensed agents, fear has you running ragged in search of legitimate opportunities, trying to grab a piece of the pie before it disappears.

The problem is, most of your leads turn out to be wild goose chases that never turn into real business. In fact, probably 80 percent of your time gets wasted on work that generates exactly zero revenue (but plenty of frustration and heartbreak).That high-cost, low-return activity is a drain on your time, energy, and bank account, but it feels like a requirement. How else are you supposed to get any clients?

So you chase, chase, chase. Convince, convince, convince. Close, close, close. Rinse and repeat.

And the solution to every problem always feels the same: just do one more deal. How many times have you said it to yourself? *If I can just do one more deal, everything will be okay.* Forget "location, location, location"—the true refrain in this business is "more, more, more."

Would it be ridiculous to say all the training you've received has been focused on how to get some version of "more" in your business? More contacts, leads, appointments, buyers, listings, sales, money, market share, rankings, time, people working for you. Fill in the blank as you like.

It's hard to not be seduced by the prospect of more. It sounds so wonderful...but it's usually a trap. More rarely solves anything. It only leads to more desire. If you do what you've been taught, you might increase your productivity, but the stress and struggle will not disappear. Ultimately, you'll be left in the same place you are now, wanting and thinking you need to do more. It's a never-ending cycle that leads to mental and emotional exhaustion.

On top of that, whether you realize it or not, every force imaginable is conspiring to turn you into a commodity. This is the biggest trap of all, and no one is immune. Industry "best practices" manipulate you into thinking that to win business, you must work harder, spend more money, give away your most valuable information, promise more than you can deliver, and charge less than you deserve. You're forced into a transactional perspective that pits your ambition against your integrity.

That's a formula for burnout if there ever was one.

THE MISSING PIECE

You know who doesn't burn out?

Tom Brady.

Even if you've never watched a single football game in your life, I bet you know who he is: the winningest quarterback in NFL history, with more Super Bowl victories (seven) than any other player *or* team. In twenty-two seasons in the NFL, he has suffered only one serious injury, and at age forty-four, he shows no signs of slowing down.

That longevity is no accident, and it has more to do with *your* longevity in real estate than you might think.

As Brady explained in his book, *The TB12 Method: How to Achieve a*

Lifetime of Sustained Peak, the normal cycle for athletes is to train, play, get hurt, and rehab, over and over. The problem is that typical fitness models emphasize strength and conditioning but are missing another crucial piece: pliability. Pliability removes the tension and stress from the training process, eliminating the main cause of injury.

- In *Never Split the Difference*, I found the missing piece for real estate agents: *Tactical Empathy*.

To explain what that means, let me back up a step. Remember, you can't overcome emotion with fact, logic, and reason...but you can work *with* those emotions to do business in a more authentic and effective way. You can learn from what works in other high-stakes, emotional situations (like the hostage negotiations Chris knows so well), and use it to make the real estate business work better for everyone—you *and* the buyers and sellers who hire you.

I can't emphasize it enough: emotion is what really drives decisions in real estate. You're shepherding buyers and sellers through one of the most stressful and significant decisions of their lives, and everyone's hopes and dreams are on the line. Buyers are hoping to find the perfect home for a bargain, and sellers are hoping to make a boatload of money on the asset they've been lovingly maintaining for years. On top of that, you want a painless deal that satisfies everyone, pays you a respectable commission, and generates repeat and referral business in the future.

But when it comes to sales training for agents, the science and skill of dealing with emotions (both yours and those of your prospects and clients) is practically nonexistent. Scripted presentations, objection handlers, and closing dialogues still rule the day. Emotional intelligence rarely gets a mention, and empathy never.

Instead, you're taught to win clients by explaining your value: your track record, market insight, pricing strategy, resources, connections, time commitment, and of course, your discounted fee. One by one, you present the factual, logical reasons why you're the best for the job...and your prospects smile and thank you profusely and never call you again. Every conversation is like an unwinnable tug-of-war: you're trying to pull them over to your side with fact, logic, and reason, but the harder you pull, the more they resist.

How many times have you left an appointment with no clue whether you had a real shot at getting the listing? How many times did you think you had it in the bag, only to find out later that they went with someone else? Why does this happen?

Because you didn't make them feel understood.

Not that you didn't understand them. I'm sure you did. You just didn't make them *feel understood*.

It's almost the same thing Stephen Covey said in *The 7 Habits of Highly Effective People*: "Seek first to understand, then to be understood." What he forgot to mention was that understanding doesn't count for anything until the *other person believes* you understand them. You know what they say when that happens?

"That's right."

As in, "That's right, you are now seeing the world from my perspective and speaking my language. You get me."

Reaching "that's right" requires **Tactical Empathy**: the art of influencing others by articulating what they're thinking and feeling, without necessarily agreeing, disagreeing, or sympathizing.

> ## Tactical Empathy
>
> The art of influencing others by articulating what they're thinking and feeling, without necessarily agreeing, disagreeing, or sympathizing.

Just as pliability removes tension from athletic training, Tactical Empathy takes the stress out of real estate sales. It cuts off the agent's doom loop before it even starts—no more endless rounds of chasing, convincing, and closing.

FROM EXPLAINING VALUE TO BUILDING TRUST

This is what no one else is teaching. It's the master key to constructing a real estate business based on building trust instead of explaining value.

When you explain your value, you become a commodity engaged in pushing transactions. Brutal, but honest.

When you cultivate trust, you become an irreplaceable advisor who creates strong relationships that yield a constant flow of repeat and referral business. Would you be opposed to hustling less while enjoying your work more and reaping bigger financial rewards? That's what trust does for you.

Forget just surviving—the methodology you're about to learn is going to make you feel alive in a brand new way. It will teach you how to become the trusted advisor your clients want, need, and will actually hire. Our approach builds on the most comprehensive scientific understanding of how people actually make decisions.

Spoiler alert: rational calculations are just the tip of the iceberg.

Below the surface are complex layers of biases, tendencies, and other brain phenomena that often make human behavior seem anything but logical. Whether you're aware of it or not (and most people aren't), these things affect your every move, from how you interpret a client's comment to what you choose to eat for lunch. Over the last few decades, researchers have tested and explained these patterns in ways that completely change how we think about influencing people.

Foreign as these ideas may be in real estate, they've already revolutionized other industries and been validated over and over by scientific studies. What you're about to learn is a more human, authentic, and honest way to sell real estate, which is precisely why it works so well.

Just imagine: what if your ambition didn't have to compete with your integrity? What if you could work in a way that aligned with your core values, beliefs, and principles? What if you could do well, be well, and help others at the same time?

Right now, you probably feel like most of what you say to your clients and prospects falls on deaf ears. When you master Tactical Empathy—the art of making people feel understood—they will finally start to hear you. Then, instead of pushing them to follow your advice, you can gently guide them in the right direction they need to go to get what they want...with them thinking it's their idea.

This book is about one simple, inescapable truth: **how you do business is more important than how much business you do.**

It sounds crazy on the surface, but you're about to see that if you focus on the *how*, the *how much* will take care of itself.

NEW NEURAL PATHWAYS

When Chris and I started coaching together in late 2017, I made an immediate 180-degree pivot in my coaching practice, incorporating Chris's knowledge into everything I taught my clients. I couldn't *not* do that—the truth is the truth. When you hear it, it is virtually impossible to resist.

It was a seismic shift. We were laying waste to the foundation of the real estate business, turning every norm upside down, and we didn't have any hard proof yet that it would work for this industry. It had to be the right direction, though. Human nature doesn't care what industry you're in.

Just enough people believed in our conviction that we could start proving the theory. It wasn't easy—a paradigm shift never is. At first, people tried to apply these new ideas to the old way of doing things, using new language to keep chasing, convincing, and closing better. That's not how this works. If you try to do it halfway, it will fail.

But when you do it right, it's rocket fuel for your business.

Our clients have shown us time and time again that this stuff transforms careers. They do more business, but more importantly, they do it in a better way. They have less stress and more time and energy. Every deal comes easier, and leaves all parties feeling happier when it's done. The tough conversations that used to keep them up at night now come effortlessly. Nobody wants to be a pushy salesperson, and what we teach allows them to leave that behind forever...and be *more* successful than they were before.

Agents come to us with all the usual struggles: how to win more clients, manage their workloads, navigate tough conversations, close deals faster, and get better outcomes from those deals. When they learn to use Tactical Empathy as the foundation for everything they do, all those problems start to solve themselves.

You'll see it in the real-life stories we've included in this book, and you'll find out firsthand when you try these strategies yourself. The beauty is that they work immediately. Unlike learning a new sport or musical instrument, you don't have to practice for months before you can be effective. As soon as you start using Tactical Empathy, people will start responding to you differently. It can literally change the course of your career overnight.

That said, this is a new skill, and you *will* feel awkward at first. It's not complicated, and it doesn't take any special genius, but learning to use it is going to be uncomfortable and unnatural. It will go against everything you think you know about how to do your job, and you're going to think there's no way this stuff will work...but it does.

Feel the fear, and commit to doing it anyway. Every time you do, you'll strengthen the new neural pathways in your brain, and if you keep at it, soon what was once very unnatural will become second nature. That's when radical change becomes not just possible, but inevitable.

This book touches on every aspect of your relationship with a client, from the first conversation to the last impression. In each chapter, we'll examine the usual way of doing things and see how Tactical Empathy turns it on its head—and leads to wildly better results. You'll get the combined benefit of my industry experience and Chris's unparalleled negotiation expertise, plus evidence from scientific studies and examples from the agents we coach.

Practice as you go, and by the end of the book, you'll never want to do business without Tactical Empathy again.

Chapter 1

IGNORE HUMAN NATURE AT YOUR PERIL

|||||||||||||||||||||||||||||||||||||||||||||||||||||||||||||||||||||||||||||||||||||||||||||||||||||||||||||||||||||||||||||||||

Starting now, you're on a mission
of fearless discovery.

|||||||||||||||||||||||||||||||||||||||||||||||||||||||||||||||||||||||||||||||||||||||||||||||||||||||||||||||||||||||||||||||||

WHERE DO YOU GO WHEN YOU'RE HIGHLY EDUCATED, EXTREMELY accomplished, and interested in making a lot of money?

Sell residential real estate? Isn't that why you bought this book? Please indulge me on a short journey...

The younger me's thought? Wall Street or Silicon Valley, the American meccas of ambition and brainpower.

Why? Those are the homes of the most important investment banks and venture capital firms, which deliberately recruit the smartest of the smarty-pants from the world's top universities. They need people who can do the sophisticated analyses required to make good investment decisions, and they pay top dollar for them. You would think that with all that talent at their disposal, fact, logic, and reason would rule the day in the investment world.

Fat chance. Just look at all the companies that have skyrocketed to massive valuations, only to collapse into nothing when the hype wears out.

Take Theranos, the company that promised to revolutionize blood testing and drug delivery. It took in over $700 million in capital and reached a valuation of $9 billion on promises alone, with no hard evidence that its core technology even worked. The investors who backed Theranos and the huge healthcare companies who partnered with it heard what they wanted to hear, and chose to believe it without fully verifying the facts.

Theranos wasn't an isolated incident, although it's certainly one of the most extreme. Emotion-driven booms and busts happened with WeWork, GameStop, SunEdison, Enron...the list is long. Investors heard and saw things that sounded so wonderful, they neglected to check their sources and crunch the numbers properly.

Here's both the good news...and the bad news. Human beings are not purely rational creatures. Yes, we're capable of logic, but our emotions and instincts are powerful enough to derail that analytical thinking, often without us even noticing. Over the past few decades, advances in neuroscience have allowed scientists to show just how active the emotional brain is during the decision process. The data on human behavior in real-life decision-making situations backs this up.

Fact, logic, and reason are just one part of how people do business, and the higher the pressure, the smaller that part often is. Make no mistake—real estate is high stakes. Buying or selling a house might be the biggest financial transaction a person ever makes, and it affects every aspect of their daily lives.

Your influence won't stick until you make them feel understood. That concept is as sure as gravity. Chris and I (and the Black Swan Group), would call it a Law of Negotiation Gravity.

The first step toward your goal of having your influence stick is to learn what's really going on inside their heads. Not the pro/con, profit/loss calculations but the emotions that so often override logical reasoning. When you understand and accept these realities of the human condition, your job (and your life) will get a lot easier.

Another of the Black Swan Group's Laws of Negotiation Gravity: "Ignore human nature at your peril."

Chris and I believe so strongly in this, that in this book and for your challenges, we are going to give you the Seven Essential Truths of Human Behavior.

SEVEN ESSENTIAL TRUTHS OF HUMAN BEHAVIOR [1]

There are whole libraries of books on human behavior, if you want to see the evidence in nitty-gritty detail. That's pretty time consuming, and you're busy, so here's a quick hit list of what you need to know, spelled out in plain English. Some of these statements may seem surprising or

---

[1] Some of these are similar to the Laws of Negotiation Gravity used by Chris Voss's Black Swan Group, and as part of the Black Swan Method. Our thinking is closely aligned with theirs, for obvious reasons. For more information, check out the Black Swan Group website at www.blackswanltd.com.

counterintuitive at first, but when you start applying them to what you see every day, you'll realize how much they explain about why people do what they do.

1. The best predictor of future behavior is past behavior.

This clichéd phrase bothers some people because they think it implies that people can't change, which isn't true. It doesn't—it just implies that it's *hard* for people to change, which is absolutely true. We're creatures of habit because doing things on autopilot makes it easier to function in a world with way more information and choices than even our advanced brains can handle.

There's an important nuance here—the word "behavior." We are not applying this truth to "words", specifically "words" compared to "behavior." There is an old saying, "Your actions shout so loudly in my ears I can't hear what you are saying."

This is one of the reasons why the "Yes Momentum" has been shown to be faulty.[2]

When was the last time you thought about the way you walk, talk, or think? How often do you buy the same things without even considering other options? How much of your day is taken up by routines of hygiene, exercise, food, work, and travel? It's not a bad thing. We *need*

---

[2] "A surprisingly large percentage (at least half) of our participants showed no strong inherent preference for consistency." Robert B. Cialdini, Melanie R. Trost, and Jason T. Newsom, "Preference for Consistency: The Development of a Valid Measure and the Discovery of Surprising Behavioral Implications," *Journal of Personality and Social Psychology* 69, no. 2 (1995): 318–328, https://doi.org/10.1037/0022-3514.69.2.318.

to minimize the cognitive demands of everyday activities so we can free up brainpower for the tough stuff.

What this does mean that in most situations, people (including you) are most likely to *do* what they've *done* in the past under similar circumstances. This is especially true under pressure—when stress hijacks most of our gray matter, we default back to our habits. Yet even in low-stress situations, people tend to stick with what they know because it feels comfortable and safe.

Just recognizing this helps you predict how people will behave. If you can find out what they did the last time they sold their house or made some other major decision, you'll have a big clue about what they're likely to do this time around.

Don't forget that this maxim applies to you too. This book is going to push you to break and rebuild your habits around selling real estate, and it's going to be uncomfortable. But the more you practice new behaviors, the more they *become* the past behaviors that you default to. The first time is the hardest—it only gets easier after that.

2. There is no such thing as a fully open mind.

In studies of B2B buyer decision-making, researchers have found that when a buyer contacts a vendor, their mind is already made up about half the time.[3] If it's not, they're more than halfway through the decision process.

---

[3] TrustRadius, *The 2021 B2B Buying Disconnect*, November 2020, https://www.trustradius.com/vendor-blog/b2b-buying-disconnect-2021?utm_source=website&utm_medium=button&utm_campaign=B2BDD2021.

The numbers are a bit shocking, but when you put yourself in the buyer's shoes, it makes perfect sense. When you make a big purchase, you don't just go straight for the salesperson. You gather information first. By the time you talk to a salesperson, you've learned enough about your options to have a pretty good idea of what you want. Your mind is no longer fully open.

Fair-minded people have a hard time embracing this. You don't want to think of yourself or others as close-minded. When you're the buyer, you tell yourself that every option is still in the running until you've made your final decision, even when you know deep down that you have a clear preference. You talk to other salespeople, thinking maybe they'll say something to sway you, but in reality, the chances of that are minuscule.

When Chris needed to hire an HR consultancy to work with his company, his accountant suggested a firm to him. He interviewed that firm and liked them, but he still talked to others to see how they might be different. He knows quite well there's no such thing as an open mind, but even he was kidding himself that he might choose someone other than his accountant's referral. Then, in the middle of a sales conversation with another candidate, he asked himself what the chances were that he would actually give that person his business. Zilch: he was always going to go with the recommendation of a trusted ally.

In the next chapter, you'll see how this changes *everything* about how you do business. It sounds like a negative thing at first—no one wants to believe they're not really in the running. In reality, though, it's the key to your freedom. If you can learn to tell when a buyer is truly considering you and when they're not, you can stop wasting your time on false opportunities.

3. Humans are hardwired to be negative.

It's right there in our brain structure. In our layman's assessment of studies we have seen of fMRI activity of the human brain in response to negative emotions, 70 percent of the amygdala (the part of your brain that assigns emotional importance to sensory information) is dedicated to negative emotions.[4]

This is pure evolutionary biology. Responding appropriately to danger with negative emotions like fear or anger is a lot more crucial to survival than responding to positive stimuli. So, it makes sense that our brains err on the side of caution—that's how you stay alive. Most of us don't face life-and-death threats every day anymore, but evolution hasn't caught up with modern civilization.

Most real estate agents are bogged down in negativity. They walk around waiting for the other shoe to drop, thinking about what bad thing is going to happen next: what tough conversation they'll have to have, what mistake they've made, what will upset the client.

We can't change our biology, but we can use simple tools to help mitigate that natural negativity. In those same fMRI studies, something fascinating happened. When the researchers asked the subjects to label their negative emotions, those emotions dissipated. They defused negativity

---

[4] Alex Korb, *The Upward Spiral: Using Neuroscience to Reverse the Course of Depression, One Small Change at a Time* (Oakland: New Harbinger Publications, 2015).

just by labeling it. In later chapters, you'll learn how to use this technique to make tough conversations with your clients a whole lot easier.

4. Fear of loss is the primary motivator of human beings.

Daniel Kahneman's Prospect Theory, which won the 2002 Nobel Prize in Economics, says that the pain of a loss is twice as powerful as the pleasure of an equivalent gain.[5] In other words, to make up for the pain of losing ten dollars, you would have to gain twenty. Financially, that puts you ten dollars ahead, but emotionally, you're even.

That means the fear of loss is a much more potent motivator than the prospect of gain. So, why is every real estate agent pitching the prospect of gain? It's a "best practice" that many people are reluctant to part with. Talking about future gain feels positive and safe; talking about potential loss feels negative and manipulative.

But in fact, the surest way to get someone to act is to make them perceive inaction as a loss. Self-help giant Tony Robbins understands this—that's why he guides people to imagine their ideal future in vivid detail, to the point where they feel like it's truly theirs. Then, if they don't take the steps required to make it real, they're *losing* that ideal future. Through visualization alone, the prospect of gain turns into the prospect of loss, and suddenly the need for action seems much stronger.

This is a crucial human foible to keep in mind when influencing clients and prospects. What seems like a complete unwillingness to

---

[5] "Loss Aversion," BehavioralEconomics.com, accessed April 8, 2022, https://www.behavioral economics.com/resources/mini-encyclopedia-of-be/loss-aversion/.

follow your advice can change in an instant when you bring a compelling prospect of loss into view.

5. Compromise is never equal—it's a downward spiral.

Everyone thinks compromise is the way to make a fair deal. You give a little, I give a little, and we come to a fair middle ground that everyone can accept, right? Even Shark Tank investor Kevin O'Leary says a good deal is one where both sides are slightly unhappy, meaning both have compromised a little.

Well, what if I can't choose between black shoes and brown shoes? Should I compromise by wearing one of each? Of course not. That's the worst possible outcome, and the same is true for real estate deals (or any negotiation).

This goes back to Prospect Theory again. Every time you give ten dollars, you won't feel satisfied until you hit the other side for twenty, and they won't feel satisfied until they hit you for forty, and on and on. It's easy to see why both sides end up unhappy with a compromise.

Whether the deal looks good on paper or not is irrelevant. What matters is that your clients *feel bad* about it, and clients who feel bad don't recommend you to others. Compromise is killing your referral rate...which kills your pipeline and your future.

6. People will die over their autonomy.

"Give me liberty or give me death." It's not just a slogan of the American Revolution—it's the expression of a simple human truth. No society has ever been content in slavery.

S.W.A.T. teams learned this the hard way in their early days, when their hostage negotiation strategy was to shout, "Come out or we'll kill you!" People are kings of their castles, and given that kind of ultimatum, they often value their autonomy over their lives. So, S.W.A.T. teams all over the country ended up shooting people who didn't need to be shot.

Even when it's not a life-or-death ultimatum, no one likes to be forced into a choice. That's why persuading in the typical sense feels so uncomfortable. You feel pushy and they feel pushed, even if what you're convincing them to do is truly in their best interest. That's no way to build trust or rapport.

In later chapters, you'll learn exactly how to influence people while allowing them to stay in the driver's seat and own their choices. It doesn't just make them happier—it will make you happier too because you won't have to feel like a sleazy salesman, or take responsibility for choices that aren't yours to make.

7. Vision drives decision.

Consciously or otherwise, everyone has visions in their mind of what they fear and want. In virtually every situation, we imagine how things will turn out before they actually happen, anchoring our expectations based on those personal (and often unspoken) desires and worries. That vision of the future determines how we act in the present.

Let's say you've just been introduced to a new skill, something that's way outside your comfort zone. It seems difficult, and you immediately imagine yourself failing at it. You haven't even tried it yet, but your mind is already fixated on the possibility of frustration, humiliation, and disappointment. So, you decide to pass altogether.

How about a scenario we're all familiar with: a seller who has a vision that their house will sell at their inflated target price. Even if you tell them the price is too high, they're anchored on that expectation and won't budge.

Before you can influence someone, you have to know what their vision is. Most agents focus on conveying and defending their own point of view, not realizing that their vision isn't the one that matters. Your clients and prospects already have their own visions of what's going to happen, and they don't care what yours is. Your job is to see their vision, and gently nudge them to adjust it when it's out of touch with reality.

TACTICAL EMPATHY®:
YOUR SWISS ARMY KNIFE

Real estate brings those seven essential truths out in everyone because it's not just a transaction—it's the American dream. Owning property is part of that glorious ideal of freedom and equality, which makes it extremely emotional. Even for seasoned home owners who have bought and sold before, the deal determines not just their next home but how the next phase of their lives will look. That's heady stuff.

Every seller is hoping for more money, and every buyer is hoping for a bargain. To get as close as possible to those dreams, they're going to need you, but they won't accept your help until they know you get what they want. They want to feel seen, heard, and understood.

Thankfully, you don't need a different tactic for each one of those seven truths. They all share one solution: Tactical Empathy. Think of Tactical Empathy as the Swiss Army knife for making people feel understood. It isn't just one tool—it's a collection of tools that work together to achieve one life-changing outcome.

To see what that outcome looks like, imagine you and a client are standing on opposite sides of the street. What most agents do is shout across the street for the other person to come over...which hardly ever works. And when they try to practice understanding or empathy, it just means using their knowledge of the client to hone their argument. They're looking for the right things to say to convince the other person to cross.

That's not Tactical Empathy. In this book, what you're learning to do is cross the street, look at what they're seeing, point out some things they might have missed, and then help them navigate to where they want to go.

Night and day, right?

Not only is it vastly more effective to do business this way, but it also feels good, thanks to the brain chemistry of trust. When people feel understood, they get a hit of oxytocin, the same hormone that bonds parents and children, romantic partners, and friends. Tactical Empathy helps you form a very real bond that will endure even through the inevitable frustrations and anxieties of getting to a deal.

THE EXPLORER MINDSET

Starting now, you're on a mission of *fearless discovery*.

There is nothing to be afraid of. None of what you're going to do is about making stuff happen—it's about embracing what's happening. You don't have to become a different person or put on a mask to be successful with this. All you have to do is set aside your desires, get curious about other people, and open yourself to being smarter today than you were yesterday.

We call this an experiment in surrendering[6]: an ongoing exercise in letting go of control and detaching yourself from the outcome of each conversation and deal.

Remember, you're not making any irrevocable decisions by trying new things. Inevitably, there will be something in this book that will violate a principle you hold dear. It's going to horrify you, and your amygdala will whisper in your ear about how it will go bad...but your amygdala is not your friend. Promise yourself now that no matter how scary it seems, you will at least try it.

You're not burning any bridges. You can always go back to your old methods if it turns out as horribly as you imagined. In our experience though, it never does.

So, don't defeat yourself before you begin. We've seen agents sit in their cars for an hour before knocking on the door, ruminating on everything that could go wrong. Why torture yourself like that? Just dive in and see what happens. It's an experiment, and you're a scientist, just observing the outcome and collecting data. No value judgment.

---

[6] Inspired in large part by Michael Singer and his book, *The Surrender Experiment*.

In those moments when it feels hard to just do it, it's helpful to think about cows and buffalo in a storm. When cows feel a storm coming, they instinctively run from it. But the storm always catches up, and they end up running right along with it, prolonging the pain and frustration. That's exactly what you're doing to yourself when you procrastinate, hesitate, and avoid the inevitable.

Buffalo, on the other hand, run straight towards the storm. By facing it head-on instead of trying to avoid it, they minimize the time they spend in the wind and rain. The hard part is over faster because they charged right into it.

So, as you practice the techniques in this book, remember that trying to avoid the tough stuff only prolongs the pain. Be the buffalo. Run into the storm.

Of course, we can't guarantee Tactical Empathy will work 100 percent of the time. Nothing does. However, Tactical Empathy will give you the best chance for success in any situation.

In Chris's experience using Tactical Empathy in hostage negotiations, his teams had a 93 percent success rate. That meant 7 percent of hostage takers were going to get shot. So, they learned to look right away for signs that the other party wasn't responding as expected.

You might find people like that, who have put up such a strong shield against empathy that they're unreceptive to this method. When you do, walk away—you don't want to work with those people. They're rare, though. Most people crave empathy, and when you learn to practice it with authenticity and confidence, you'll find that virtually everyone around you will light up in response—prospects, clients, colleagues, and even your friends and family.

That's when you'll realize this is more than a way of doing business. It's a way of living. It's a reawakening of who you really are as a human being.

It just happens to also help you build a stronger business. And now that you've seen the essential truths of how people behave, you can put that knowledge to work, starting with the very first conversation you have with a prospect.

KEY TAKEAWAYS

➔ Fact, logic, and reason are only a small part of how people make decisions. Emotions and unconscious biases play a huge role, and often make human behavior seem irrational.

➔ You'll have an easier time understanding and predicting people if you remember these Seven Essential Truths of Human Behavior:

   ▷ The best predictor of future behavior is past behavior.

   ▷ There is no such thing as a fully open mind.

   ▷ Humans are hardwired to be negative.

   ▷ Fear of loss is the primary motivator of human beings.

   ▷ Compromise is never equal—it's a downward spiral.

   ▷ People will die over their autonomy.

   ▷ Vision drives decision.

➔ Tactical Empathy is your Swiss Army knife for navigating human relationships and behavior.

➔ As you learn to practice it throughout this book, approach the process with an attitude of fearless discovery. There's nothing to be afraid of here, and the discomfort of trying new things will disappear faster if you dive in head first.

Chapter 2

THE FAVORITE OR THE FOOL

It's not a sin to lose business—it's a sin to take a long time to lose business.

ONCE UPON A TIME IN A MAGICAL, MYSTICAL REAL ESTATE MARKET, there lived an incredible real estate agent.

She was truly on top of her game.

She cultivated the right mindset, built strong relationships, and out-worked everyone. Everything in her business was buttoned up tight and state of the art. She was the personification of best practices for a real estate professional.

One day, she received a phone call from a potential seller who asked her to come out and give a listing presentation. It was the perfect opportunity for the agent—this property and client fit her ideal profile for doing business.

The agent prepared everything diligently, as always. She dropped off a pre-listing package, confirmed the appointment in advance, and arrived on time, ready to go with a big smile and positive attitude. It was show time!

The meeting could not have gone more perfectly. The prospective sellers listened to everything she said, seemed very engaged, and asked very specific questions. Their attention never faded during the two-hour presentation.

The sellers thanked the agent profusely and commented on how impressed they were with everything she had shared. They said with a big smile, "You've given us so much to think about. Let us process everything, and we'll get back to you shortly."

The agent left the meeting on cloud nine. She desperately wanted this listing, and knew she was the best person for the job. Given that the appointment had gone even better than expected, it seemed like a sure thing. She started going through her database mentally, thinking of who she might show the property to. This was going to be fun, not to mention a great paycheck.

The next day, the phone rang. It was the seller on the line, and the agent's heart started beating rapidly in anticipation of good news...that never came.

The sellers shared again how grateful they were for all the information the agent had presented, but they had decided to work with someone else. The agent was in shock, and could barely say thank you for the call. She hung up the phone in absolute disbelief.

This made no sense. She had done everything right from start to finish. She was the obvious choice. What could have possibly happened? Did she say something wrong? Did she totally misread the situation?

This is the story of the Favorite and the Fool.

This version involves made-up people in a nonexistent place, but you already know it's a true story because it has happened to you (probably more times than you can count). And if you're like most agents, you're still wondering what you did wrong.

Just one thing: you assumed you actually had a shot in the first place.

You probably think I'm crazy for saying that. Of course you had a shot! Why else would they have called you and asked for a listing presentation?

What you're about to learn is that not all opportunities are created equal. Sometimes you have a high probability of doing business with a prospective client—you're the Favorite. Other times (far too often), you're the Fool. Someone else is already the Favorite, and you're just there for due diligence...wasting your time on work that will never lead to a deal, no matter what you say or do.

The key to building a great business is learning to tell the difference between possibility and probability. Fools chase possibilities. To be the Favorite, you have to focus on probabilities.

The concept of the Favorite and the Fool is the main organizing principle in this book. Everything else flows from this fundamental distinction. How you approach your real estate business (and the results you get from it) will change dramatically once you embrace this reality.

This is a tough pill for most agents to swallow. You're probably pushing back on this idea right now. Everyone wants to believe that if they say and do the right things, every seller will hire them, but it's simply not true.

Still skeptical? Keep reading. In this chapter, you'll see how one faulty assumption—that the playing field is level—wreaks havoc on your business every single day. More importantly, you'll learn how focusing on high-probability opportunities can transform your life, and how to start doing that *today*.

THE OLD WAY: CHASE, CONVINCE, CLOSE

Ask yourself if any of this sounds familiar:

You get excited about every phone call from a new prospect.

On those calls, your primary objective is to get a listing appointment.

You think that the more listing appointments you go on, the more listings you'll get.

You believe prospects are making decisions based on the quality of your listing presentations, so you put a lot of time, effort, energy, and resources into them.

You know not every appointment will result in a listing, but you consider that a cost of doing business.

You chase every opportunity that crosses your path because if you don't, you might not get anything at all.

The vast majority of real estate agents think this way, so I don't blame you for doing the same. Unfortunately, it's all wrong.

Chris and I coach agents who now go on *zero* listing appointments and do more business than ever. It's not because they're superstars who are so in demand that they can afford not to do the work that "regular" people have to do. It's because they've accepted and adapted to a reality of the human condition: there's no such thing as a fully open mind[7].

The truth is, most people who contact you have no intention of ever hiring you.

They're not being deceptive or manipulative on purpose. They *think* their minds are open. But as soon as they start gathering information to make a decision, they begin to lean towards certain choices, and away from others. They start to pick a Favorite, maybe even unconsciously. Most top agents believe they are going to walk away from every listing appointment with a signed listing. Most newer agents are just happy to get a phone call. The idea that the seller has already made a decision (or is close to it) never crosses their mind.

When you're the Favorite, chances are very high (probably 80 percent or better) that you'll get the listing. It's not because of your killer presentation, though. The prospect picked you before you ever walked into that house, whether they realized it or not.

When you're not the Favorite, you're the Fool—and there is always a fool in the game. The prospect is interviewing multiple agents because it's the responsible thing to do, but it's just due diligence. They might even use the ideas and information you provide, but the chances of swaying them away from their Favorite are low (maybe 20 percent at best), even if you say and do all the right things.

---

[7] One of the Seven Essential Truths of Human Behavior.

Twenty percent isn't zero, though, and there's the danger. Sometimes, you'll win one of these low-probability listings, and that makes you believe that you can *convince* people to choose you. You start to think that if you can just make your presentation a little better—more polished, more exciting, more insightful, more packed with reasons why you're the best—you'll persuade more people to hire you. But convincing is hard work, and it doesn't feel good for you or them.

Would you rather go on a date with someone who is thrilled to be with you, or someone you had to beg? Which situation would make you feel more confident and relaxed? Which would be more enjoyable and more likely to end well?

Now, put yourself in their shoes. Would you rather go on a date with your crush, or someone who wore you down until you couldn't say no? Which date are you more likely to walk into with a positive outlook? Which person are you more likely to forgive for a little mistake or imperfection?

If you have to convince someone to work with you, chances are high that they'll have a bad attitude, unreasonable expectations, and little mercy. Your relationship with them is weak from the get-go. After the hard work of convincing them to hire you, you'll have an even harder time convincing them to trust and respect you. When you hit the bumps that are inevitable in every real estate transaction, you'll be the one feeling the pain.

Marketing guru Joe Polish calls those clients HALFs®: hard, annoying, lame, and frustrating. (The *L* could stand for lucrative, which these clients sometimes are, but that money is hard earned indeed.)

> ## The Connected:
> ## Joe Polish & Genius Network
>
> Joe Polish is one of the most connected people on earth and the founder of Genius Network, a phenomenal network of entrepreneurs. Check it out at www.geniusnetwork.com.

When you're the Fool, life is rough.

THE NEW WAY:
HIGH-PROBABILITY ACTIVITY

Fortunately, the solution is simple: find out whether you're the Favorite or the Fool as fast as possible, and if you're not the Favorite, *walk away*. You're probably thinking that sounds incredibly scary, but bear with me.

There are two kinds of phone calls you'll get in your business. One is, "We're gonna sell, and we want you to list our home." The other is, "We're interviewing agents."

Build your business around the first call.

This is about stacking the odds in your favor. As Chris says, we live in a Las Vegas world, and not all the games give you the same chance of success. That first call is a table where your odds of winning are 80 percent. At the other table, your odds are just 20 percent. Which table do you want to sit at?

The answer seems obvious, but in reality, you've probably spent most of your career at that low-probability table: chasing and convincing, chasing and convincing, over and over, hoping and praying that someone will eventually pick you. You've seen how well that works. This book is about choosing to focus on high-probability activity instead. From now on, you're going to sit at the 80 percent table.

When you embrace the concept of the Favorite or the Fool, everything gets simplified. You no longer have to walk around on eggshells, worrying whether someone will work with you or not, fearful of saying or doing the wrong thing. When you're the Favorite, clients will commit to you up front, so there's no wondering or guessing. It's a magical thing.

When you do meet the prospective seller in their living room, it's not a listing appointment where you're trying to win them over with your valuable insights, which they may or may not swipe and use some other agent. Instead, it's a strategy meeting with paying clients who are already receptive to your advice. Building trust is natural, the work is more enjoyable, and the bumps in the road are easier to handle.

As Joe Polish puts it, those clients are ELFs®: easy, lucrative, and fun.

Best of all, those clients are far more likely to hire you repeatedly and refer people to you. That's the key to building the strong, reliable, profitable business you're dreaming of. We all know that repeat and referral business is the true gold mine of real estate, and now you know why: because you're already the Favorite. The more often you're the Favorite, the more often you *will be* the Favorite in the future. It's a virtuous cycle with the power to transform your entire career and life. Repeat and referral business is the low hanging fruit in real estate. Stop making the rookie mistake of not nurturing relationships on a daily basis.

Now, here's the part you're not going to like. You're going to resist this with every fiber of your being because it goes against what you've always believed about how to succeed in business.

To make room for high-probability activity, you have to say *NO* to everything else. (Gently, of course—we'll get to that later in this chapter.)

That's right—I'm telling you to let all those other opportunities pass you by. Turn them down, even though you may have a 20 percent chance of converting. Let them go. Save yourself the time, money, and heartache. They weren't going to go well for you anyway.

The FOMO is going to kick in hard here, but you've got to fight past it. That fear is lying to you. It's saying there aren't enough opportunities where you're the Favorite, and if you start passing things up, you won't do enough deals. Your business will fail. You'll lose everything. You'll starve. *You'll die.*

This is the place where your mind actually goes. Be ready for it. If you don't believe me, pay close attention to your self-talk next time you're in a competitive situation. You'll be shocked at the nonsense that takes place in your head.

But no, you're not going to die.

It's just your limbic brain—home of the survival instinct—blowing things out of proportion. The idea of giving up opportunities feels like a threat, so your brain revs up your anxiety, preparing you to fight, fly, or freeze. This isn't a saber-toothed tiger lurking in the bushes, ready to kill you, but your brain can't tell the difference.

As hard as it is to believe, even if you are the Favorite with only one or two out of ten people, there is still an abundance of business to do. There is never a lack of opportunity, only a lack of awareness, focus, and effort. When you make being the Favorite your standard for doing business, this choice will compound to your advantage in ways you never dreamed possible.

We've seen this play out time after time among the agents we coach. Choosing high-probability activity over low-probability activity is one of the first changes they have to make, and for most, it's an extremely challenging transition. It feels like you're going to lose business, and you might remember from Chapter 1 that human beings fear loss twice as much as they desire equivalent gains.

The truth is, the only things my agents have lost are dead-end prospects and bad clients. What they gain is more time, more peace of mind, easier work, happier clients, and more repeat and referral business.

See? There's truly nothing to fear about refusing to play the Fool. Here's what you should really be afraid of: if you waste your time playing the Fool for everyone, you might miss the chance to be someone's Favorite.

WHICH ONE ARE YOU?

It only takes one conversation to know if you're the Favorite or the Fool. Chris and I call this process *getting proof of life*, which is what hostage negotiators do first to make sure the other party isn't yanking their chain. But instead of finding out if the hostage is really there and still breathing, you want to know if there's truly a deal here, and if so, whether it's going to be with you.

It's a **cold read**, just like what I used to do on the football field. Before each game, we would study the scouting report on our opponents. We had to learn everything backwards and forwards: all their stats and tendencies based on the down, distance, formation, field position, and a number of other factors. Knowing what the other team was likely to do in any given situation helped stack the odds in our favor come gametime. Our ability to anticipate just by reading the situation in front of us could be the difference between making the play and not making the play.

Tool: The Cold Read

Paying close attention to the other person's words, tone, and body language to recognize patterns and predict their future behavior.

It's no different when you're in front of a potential seller or buyer. The clues as to whether you are the Favorite or the Fool are right there. The question is, do you recognize them? Do you know what sellers say and do when you're the Favorite? What about when you're the Fool? Being able to read the situation correctly is the difference between spending your time wisely or foolishly.

Some call this intuition, but it's really just pattern recognition, and humans are hardwired to excel at it. You have this ability already—you just need to hone it. Prospects act one way when you're the Favorite, another when you're the Fool. The more you practice reading these patterns, the easier it will be to tell the difference.

The following five questions will give you a solid framework to figure out whether you're the Favorite or Fool with each prospect. To be clear, these are questions you're asking *yourself*, not the prospect. *Don't* ask them these questions directly—we'll explain exactly what to say to get to the answers, using the Black Swan Method.[8] You'll see how prospects reveal the answers in the way they talk with you. The more confirmations you get, the more likely you're the Favorite.

1. Are they calling me specifically (or just agents)?

When talking to a prospect, the temptation is to jump straight into the sell. You want to tell them why they should work with you, why you could do the best job helping them sell or buy a home.

Don't. Instead, ask *them* to tell *you* why they want to work with you.

This is the first application of a principle that will come back later in the book: it matters who says it. When you explain why you're the right person for the job, you're convincing. When you let them explain it, you're putting their needs first and respecting their autonomy (which, as you learned in Chapter 1, people will die over).

---

[8] Developed by Chris Voss and his team at The Black Swan Group, www.blackswanltd.com.

So, ask the question: "I'm curious—of all the agents you know, why me?"

Tone of voice and pacing is critical. Go slow and be genuinely curious. Practice this line over and over again. Record yourself.

Now, listen to their answer...*without* hope in your heart. Don't think about what you're hoping to hear—just listen to what you're *actually* hearing. Are the reasons specific? Do they know who you are, or did they just call on a whim after seeing your number on a lawn sign or in a Google search result?

Their answer to this question tells you exactly how they view your value proposition. The more they know about you and can articulate their reasons for calling you specifically (not just any agent), the more likely you're the Favorite. A real answer is something you can label, mirror, and paraphrase.

Vague answers are a clue that you're the Fool in the game. They might even turn the question around on you and say, "You tell me why I should hire you." That's a big, waving red flag.

The "Why me?" question is so powerful that we have yet to see it fail to reveal whether an agent is the Favorite or the Fool. This is the prospect's chance to defend why they want to hire you. If you're the Favorite, they'll tell you. If you're not, they'll evade the question.

2. Do I fit the profile?

Here comes another throwback to Chapter 1: the best predictor of future behavior is past behavior. If they've ever bought or sold a home before, how did they pick their agent then? Was it based on a referral? Testimonials? Company affiliation? Some other factor?

Finding out how people have made big decisions in the past will help you understand how they are likely to choose an agent. There is probably a profile of the type of person that works best for them, and you want to evaluate whether you're a good match. For example, if they found their last agent through a personal connection, and you're a total stranger, the chances that they'll go with you are slim. The better you fit the profile, the more likely you're the Favorite.

Hint: If they have worked with another real estate agent in the past, be sure to find out whether they plan on working with that agent again. Instead of simply asking if they will, ask why they *wouldn't*: "Why would you not use the agent you worked with before?"

Here are some other questions you can ask to help clarify the profile:

What do you want in an agent?
How have you made decisions like this in the past?
How will you know when you've met the right person?
What guidance are you getting on this decision?
How do you see this process unfolding?

Again, listen carefully to their answers without fear and hope. Do you fit the profile of the agent they're looking for?

3. Can I make an emotional connection?

Now, can you get inside their head and read their mind? What you're looking for here is a "that's right" response.

Not "you're right," but *that's right.*

We call that a two-millimeter shift: the difference seems small on the surface, but the consequences are massive. "You're right" is what someone says when they're caving to persuasion, or giving you a polite no or a false yes. "That's right" is what they say when they feel understood, which is the ultimate goal of everything in this book.

> ## Two-millimeter Shift:
> ## "You're right" ➜ "That's right"
>
> "You're right" means they feel defensive and resistant. "That's right" means they feel understood.

To get to "that's right," you'll use two essential tools from the Tactical Empathy toolbox: labeling and mirroring.

Labeling is stating what the other person is thinking, feeling, or doing—putting a label on it. A label starts with one of these phrases:

It sounds like...

It seems like...

It feels like...

You're probably thinking...

You're probably feeling...

It ends with your best guess about what they're actually thinking and feeling. You want to get inside the other person's head and heart, to see the world from their perspective. That requires deep listening. You can't be thinking about what you are going to say next. Your full attention needs to focus on the other person and where they're coming from.

Tool: Labeling

Stating what the other person is thinking, feeling, or doing, using a phrase like "It seems like..." or "You're probably thinking/ feeling..."

To them, your labeling feels like mindreading, and that builds trust. When you can clearly articulate what someone is thinking and feeling, they'll be much more open in their communications because they hear you "get it." This concept will come back again in future chapters.

Here are a few examples of labeling with a potential client:

It sounds like you have a very specific price in mind...

It seems like selling in a timely fashion is very important to you...

It feels like this is going to be a very emotional process for you...

You're probably thinking that your home will sell very quickly...

You're probably feeling frustrated with the number of showings on your property so far...

The interesting thing about labeling is that it doesn't matter if your label is right. If it is, you'll probably get "that's right" from the other person.

If it's not, they won't be annoyed. They'll just give you more information to correct your misinterpretation. In fact, intentional mislabeling can be a very effective way to get someone to reveal more. People love to correct you when your label is wrong—for them, fixing it feels good.

Mirroring goes hand in hand with labeling. To do it, just repeat the last few words the other person just said.

Seller: We want to sell our home quickly.

Mirror: Quickly?

Seller: Yes, we want to be sold and closed by the end of summer.

Mirror: End of summer?

Mirroring gives you more clarity on what someone is saying. It takes the place of just guessing, or saying something like "Tell me more," or "Can you be more specific?" It's a powerful tool for getting people to express their thoughts and feelings more fully.

Tool: Mirroring

Repeating the last few words the other person just said, which often prompts them to expand on that train of thought.

Warning: Mirroring can feel very awkward at first. You'll probably feel like you're mimicking. Push past the discomfort and you'll quickly see the value of this tool. The more people open up and share, the more trust you create.

With both labels and mirrors, there's another two-millimeter shift going on: **"I" to "you."**

Most agents are constantly in "I" mode, making every conversation about what *they* think and feel. See for yourself—record and listen back to your client calls. Check your emails. It's "I," "I," "I" all over the place...but your interactions with clients and prospects are not about *you*. When you use "I," the other party is tuning you out.

Labels and mirrors shift you into "you" mode. They force you to concentrate on what the *other person* is thinking and feeling. To use these tools successfully, with the right tone and pacing, you have to come from a place of curiosity about the other person, not your own hope and fear. Suddenly, you're no longer talking about yourself and trying to steer the conversation in the direction you want. Instead, you're listening to them and talking about their concerns, needs, and desires.

Two-millimeter Shift:
"I" → "You"

When you're using "I," you're focused on yourself. Use labels and mirrors to shift your attention back to the other person.

People can't hear you until they feel heard. They won't understand you until they feel understood. That's Tactical Empathy 101, the fundamental stuff that no one has taught you before. When you actually start doing it, it's money in the bank.

If you can use these tools to make the other person feel understood, you've created an emotional connection, and that's a very good sign that you might be the Favorite.

4. Is the conversation collaborative?

Another good sign is when the conversation is two-way—both you and the prospect are giving and receiving information. The opposite of this is the classic "picking your brain" scenario, when they call to get information out of you and aren't willing to give any in return.

The pricing conversation is the best example of this. If you say, "It sounds like you have a specific price in mind," and they answer you directly, that's a good sign that you're the Favorite because they're not afraid to share information with you.

If you're the Fool, they'll keep their cards close. They'll say, "I don't know. You're the expert. That's why we're calling you."

How annoying is that response? It's total nonsense. You know it and they know it. Every seller has a price in mind. They might not know if it's realistic, but it's there.

In this case, the most effective label for getting them to open up is: "It sounds like you have a very specific number in mind." If they still want to be evasive, try these:

You probably have looked on Zillow...

Zillow shows a price of $_____ ...

You probably think that's low...

You're probably thinking closer to $_____ ... (Here you give a much higher price, which will trigger the seller to say, "No, not that much.")

The more you struggle to get straight answers about their target price and other important pieces of information, the more likely you're the Fool. When you're the Favorite, people will converse with you in an honest way, and not be evasive or stingy with their responses.

5. Are they opposed to making a commitment up front?

This is the toughest part of this whole process. It's where the rubber meets the road. You're going to think this will never work because everyone around you is doing the exact opposite. You'll think that no client in their right mind will agree to this.

Don't go see the property until the client has committed to working with you.

I know, every other agent is willing to go out and give a listing presentation with no commitment whatsoever. They spend hours researching the property and preparing for the appointment, then more hours driving out there and having that conversation. All on spec, with no assurance that they'll ever get anything in return.

Some call that selling, but we call it free consulting, and it's killing your business. The more value you give away for free, the less valuable

THE FAVORITE OR THE FOOL

you are. Let me repeat this, because you have built your entire real estate career on a false premise.

The more value you give away for free, the less valuable you are. Why does someone need to work with you when you have given them your entire playbook at no charge? They have what they need, and will just go back to their Favorite to make sure they're doing all the things you suggested. How often does a seller take your price, or your staging suggestions, or your marketing ideas, and list with another agent? Would I be wrong to think this has happened more than once or twice in your career?

Plus, the more time and energy you waste on listing appointments you'll never win, the less you have for the people who actually want to work with you. So, *no more free consulting* (we'll come back to this in Chapter 4).

If you're the Favorite, getting a commitment won't be an issue. The prospect knows they want to work with you, and will gladly commit before seeing your analysis of the property because they trust your expertise.

If you're the Fool, you'll see that refusing to be the victim—declining to give the prospect valuable information for free—sometimes provokes an aggressive response. They might try to pressure you by saying things like "It sounds like you don't want my business." These attacks just reveal that person as a predator. Predators attack people who refuse to be victimized. If you think back to prospects who have given you a hard time, you'll recognize this behavior.

Don't take it personally, get upset, or let them sway you. Instead, exit the situation gracefully: "It sounds like you already have a few good agents to choose from. Why don't you meet with them, and if none of them work out, you can always reach out to me again."

IT'S OKAY TO WALK AWAY

Everyone else is out there obsessing over their listing presentation, but the truth is, the whole thing is a farce. Sellers act like their minds are open, and they probably even believe it, but you know better now. They already had a Favorite before they even called you, and no listing presentation will change that.

I say it like it's obvious, but I know it's not. I spent the first twenty-five years of my coaching career teaching listing presentations. But when I found out (thanks to Chris) that it was all a waste of time, I changed my strategy in a heartbeat. In the five years since then, one truth has proven itself a million times over.

It's not a sin to lose business—it's a sin to take a long time to lose business.

Having a prospect get upset and walk away because you won't do a listing appointment is fine. Investing eight hours or more into a listing appointment and not getting hired is not fine. Convincing a client to hire you, and later walking away or getting fired because you couldn't meet their unreasonable demands is *not fine*.

That's why it's so important to answer all five of these questions in the very first conversation with each prospect. When you're just starting to practice this, it might take thirty minutes or even an hour to suss out whether you're the Favorite or the Fool. Over time, you'll get more and more efficient, until you can do it in under fifteen minutes.

Imagine that. Instead of wasting a whole day or more on each prospect and still having no idea what they'll do, you can spend just fifteen minutes finding out whether you have a serious shot or not.

That's life changing.

KEY TAKEAWAYS

→ By the time prospects call you, you're either the Favorite or the Fool. Your only goal is to find out which one.

→ Develop your cold reading skills to spot patterns of behavior that indicate you're the Favorite. Your chances are high if:

 ▷ they called you specifically and can articulate why,

 ▷ you fit the profile of people they've worked with before,

 ▷ you connect emotionally with them,

 ▷ it's a two-way conversation, and

 ▷ they're willing to commit up front to working with you.

→ Only play at the table where the odds are in your favor. If you're the Fool, walk away gracefully before you waste any more time.

Tactical Empathy Toolbox

→ **Cold Reading:** Paying close attention to the other person's words, tone, and body language to recognize patterns and predict their future behavior.

→ **Labeling:** Stating what the other person is thinking or feeling, using a phrase like "It seems like..." or "You're probably thinking/ feeling..."

→ **Mirroring:** Repeating the last few words the other person just said, which often prompts them to expand on that train of thought.

Chapter 3

NO MORE FREE CONSULTING

*Your only real value is the trust
you build with a client.*

IF YOU HAD HBO IN THE EARLY 2000S, YOU MIGHT HAVE WATCHED a show called Entourage, which revolved around an up-and-coming actor, Vincent Chase (played by Adrian Grenier), and his troublemaking friends.

Early in the series, Vincent goes looking for an agent to represent him in Hollywood. When he sits down in the first presentation, the agent shows a video that flashes one massive brand name after another: "Mercedes... Coca Cola...Vincent Chase. We intend to make you as popular as both of them." He's impressed.

At the next agency, he sits down, and it's the same thing. "Apple... Cannon...Vincent Chase." Vinny raises his eyebrows at his friend, clearly thinking, *This is the same thing we just sat through.*

At the third agency, it's the same spiel again: "Microsoft...McDonald's ...Vincent Chase...brand name recognition. What do you think?" This time, Vinny just walks out.

This is exactly what happens in the real estate industry.

Agents obsess over their listing presentations. They think that's how they win clients, so they pour effort into making their presentation marginally better than the next agent's. If you're focused on convincing prospects to choose you with facts, logic, and reason, the only way to differentiate yourself is to pack in more information and insight than anyone else. You give your time and value for free, hoping it will make you attractive enough for them to decide to pay you.

Agents call this a best practice, but they're kidding themselves. It's only a common practice masquerading as something more. Just because everyone else is jumping off a cliff doesn't make it a good idea.

You already know the logistical problems with this strategy. It takes hours, sometimes days, to do all the work involved in preparing, delivering, and following up on a listing presentation. If you don't get the job, that's a *lot* of wasted time. Plus, it's all too easy for the prospect to simply hand your playbook to the agent they wanted to work with in the first place. Your so-called competitive advantage is impossible to protect when you give it away like that.

And even with all that work, how is your listing presentation really any different from those of your top competitors? Are there any big secrets to the process of selling a home? I've sat in on hundreds of listing presentations, and while the style can vary, the substance rarely does. Real estate isn't rocket science. You can't set yourself apart with your pricing or staging or marketing tactics because everyone with a lick of sense will do it pretty much the same way.

The truth is, there's only one way to create a competitive advantage that's effective and lasting, and it has nothing to do with your value. None of the things you can put down on paper as reasons you're better than the next agent play into this. It's not about what you do but *how* you do it.

The only real way to differentiate yourself is with trust.

Trust is what makes a person choose you. It's what opens their mind to your influence, and it's what allows them to handle the bumps in the road without blaming you for every pothole. It's what leads to deals that feel good, even when they're not exactly what the client imagined at the beginning of the process. It's what makes them come back to you in the future, and refer other people to you. It's the foundation of a real estate business that's not just successful—it's sustainable.

In this chapter, you'll learn why trust is so much more powerful than value, and how to start building it from the very first moment you meet a prospect. It will go against every instinct you have as a salesperson... but *with* every instinct you have as a human being.

THE OLD WAY: EXPLAIN YOUR VALUE

Every salesperson gets trained to define the value of their products and services for their customers. It makes perfect sense—before someone will give you money for something, they need to understand how it will benefit them.

You know it's true because you shop that way. When you're comparing yogurt brands in the grocery store, or deciding whether to shell out thousands for an elite professional development course, you look for those indications of value. Which one is better? Is it worth the money?

So, when you're selling your services, you try to communicate what makes *you* better than the others and worth the money. You talk about your track record, your market insight, your pricing strategy, your resources, your connections, your time commitment, and of course, your discounted fee. Maybe you deeply believe these things bring better results to your clients than what other agents can offer.

You say all this imagining the prospect will do some kind of mental math to figure out which agent will get them the best results. That's what a logical, reasonable person would do, right?

There's just one problem. To do that, they would have to take everything you say on faith. Even if what you claim is objectively true in your mind, your prospects can't possibly have the knowledge or experience to verify that. And, just because you sell a ton of homes doesn't mean working with you will be a good experience for them. Bottom line, they have no idea if you'll actually do the things you promise, or if they'll work.

There's simply no way to know in advance which agent will get them the best results. Choosing a real estate agent isn't like buying a laptop. With a laptop, you can look at the specs and try the machines for a few minutes to get a very accurate idea of which one will work best for you.

Not so with a real estate agent—you're, as the economists put it, an experiential product. It's impossible to know the benefits of working with you without actually working with you. Not only can prospects not know ahead of time which agent will be best, but they will *never* know for sure which would have been best, not even after the deal is done. They can't go back in time and see what would have happened if they had sold the same house under the same conditions with a different agent.

So, based on your value, you're indistinguishable from other agents—you're a commodity. And you know what commodities compete on? Price.

Of all the factors that make up your value as you've presented it to your prospects, the only one they can understand and verify is your fee. So, that ends up being what they focus on, even if you know it's not the biggest factor in how much money they'll take home when the deal is done. Competing on price isn't a sustainable way to run your business because there's always someone out there who will work for less or promise more.

Most agents I meet are stuck deep in this way of doing business, commoditizing themselves by focusing on articulating their value in the listing presentation. Occasionally, though, I'll find someone who relies on the force of their personality rather than the content of the listing presentation to win clients. They think that what truly sets them apart from other agents is *them*—their personality and how they interact with their clients.

That's getting closer to the truth.

THE NEW WAY: BUILD TRUST

You can't overcome emotion with fact, logic, and reason.

Remember that, from the very beginning of this book? People make decisions based on emotions. Fact, logic, and reason are how they justify the decision after the fact. When it's impossible for a prospect to know your objective value, all they have left to go on is how they *feel* about you.

Don't forget, they're putting the biggest financial transaction of their lives in your hands. So, when I say "how they feel," it's not about whether they'd want to have a drink with you or be your friend. It's about whether they believe in your competence, honesty, and reliability. They want to know if they can *trust you* to make this a good experience for them.

Your only real value is the trust you build with a client.

Buying or selling a home is a stressful, emotional transaction, and there will be bumps in the road. Your clients will forgive you for those and let you guide them only if they trust you to protect their interests.

When they do, every aspect of the relationship works better. You can be more transparent with each other, collaborate more effectively, and get things done faster. They'll worry and nag you less, and you'll bring a more positive attitude to every interaction. The process won't be miraculously problem free, but each problem will feel more solvable and less stressful for both you and your client.

When you do a listing presentation the usual way, it does nothing to build that trust. You're just explaining about yourself and what you plan to do, not getting to know the other person and making them feel understood. Not building a relationship.

Two-millimeter Shift:
Value ➜ Trust

When you sell your value, you become a commodity engaged in transactions. When you cultivate trust, you build relationships that lead to successful deals, repeat business, and referrals.

Let's be clear: I'm not talking about cultivating trust as a tactic to win over prospects. Remember from the last chapter, there's no winning anyone over. By the time they call you, you're already the Favorite or the Fool. Their mind is made up. This chapter is not—I repeat, *not*—about swapping building trust for explaining value as a method of convincing someone to choose you.

It's about *no longer trying to convince anyone at all.*

If you're the Favorite, focusing on trust from the get-go starts the relationship off on the right foot. If you're the Fool, it leaves them with a positive feeling about you, so they'll be inclined to speak highly of you, and even come back to you if things don't work out with their Favorite. It cannot magically turn you from the Fool into the Favorite—nothing can, and the whole point of the concept is that you shouldn't try.

That said, let's talk about how to build trust.

THE INDIRECT ROUTE IS FASTER

Trust develops over time. You know this instinctively because you've built trust before. Look at all the people you trust in your life—did any of them gain that status instantaneously? Of course not. Trust builds incrementally over many conversations and shared experiences in which the other person repeatedly shows that they understand you, care about you, and will protect your interests.

That gradual process forces you to change your orientation as an agent. Instead of prioritizing short-term results, you have to focus on the long-term process. Instead of making yourself a commodity, you have to be a human being. Instead of convincing someone, you have to let them choose.

This is the indirect route.

It feels less efficient. It seems like it will take longer. But, it's like taking the ring road around a city instead of plowing through downtown traffic—less direct but much more effective. When you take the time to build trust first, everything that follows will be better and easier.

The key to building trust is letting go of your feelings and desires.

Your anxiety about whether they like you...your frustration that they're not listening to you...your hope for a smooth sale and a healthy commission...all that, and whatever other inner feelings and desires are yammering for your attention, has to go. Detach yourself from the outcome.

It's hard at first. We're all used to hearing and following that inner

NO MORE FREE CONSULTING

voice all day long. *I want this. I don't want that. I like this. I dislike that. I wish...I fear...I hope...*blah, blah, blah.

That voice is the roadblock to trust, and it's going to take some effort to learn to ignore it. Once you do, though, you'll never want to go back. You'll look back at your old, self-interested tactics, and they'll feel so dirty.

Two-millimeter Shift:
Controlling ➜ Letting Go

Talking is for chasing and convincing. Listening is for building trust. The way you listen has much more impact than anything you say or do.

It took a painful loss and some massively high stakes for me to learn to detach myself from the outcome. I wasn't drafted into the NFL— I was a free agent, and my only chance at getting signed was to go to training camp with the Miami Dolphins and hope I made the cut. They brought in ninety guys, and had to narrow the field to forty-five by the end of camp.

We practiced twice a day, and I was lucky if I'd get in four plays in an entire day. When the preseason games came, though, I got to play a lot, and I excelled. When the time came for the last cut, I did the math, and thought I had it made...but I was wrong. I was one of the very last cuts.

THE FULL FEE AGENT

To get that close to my childhood dream and have it slip away was like having my heart ripped out and stomped on. I went back to my hotel room after being cut, closed the drapes, and sat in the dark having a pity party while I listened to the celebration of the guys who made the team. Pretty sad stuff.

Then, a miracle happened. The next day, I got a knock on my door. One of the forty-five final players was put on injured reserve, so a roster spot had opened up, and I was back on the team.

But in those twenty-four hours of misery, all my confidence and bravado had gone out the window. Now, I simply didn't want to make a mistake and get cut again. I knew what it felt like to lose my dream, and I was *not* going to let it happen a second time.

So, for the first five games of the season, I was no longer playing with reckless abandon, as I had done in the preseason. Now I was playing it safe, not taking risks and not putting myself out there. I was too worried about being cut again.

Before the sixth game of the season, I got a real wake up call. We were playing the New York Jets that week, and as I walked out to practice, Coach Shula was right in front of me. He spun around, looked me square in the eye, and said, "Son, you are not doing what we put you on this team to do." Then, he turned back and walked away.

The message was obvious: I was about to get cut again. In that moment, I made a life-changing choice. I stopped in my tracks, got very quiet, and decided I was going to give my best effort and let the outcome be whatever it was going to be.

If my best effort was good enough to keep my spot on the team, great.

If not, that would be okay too. Either way, my intent and focus was crystal clear: give my best effort, and don't be attached to the outcome. This moment has never left me, and this lesson has proven invaluable, as it will for you if you choose to learn from it.

Go out every day and give your best effort, and let the score take care of itself.

Most of us run around every day grasping for control over all the things we think are happening to us. News flash: life isn't happening to you. It's just happening. You're not in control of what happens, only of how you experience it.

Agents tear themselves up all the time with the illusion that they have control. When they get the listing, they think they did something right, and when they don't, they think they did something wrong.

What if you stop trying to force the outcome you want, and just see what happens? That's where trust begins.

IF YOU'RE EXPLAINING, YOU'RE LOSING

Something incredible happens when you detach from the outcome, and ignore that voice in your head that's constantly nattering about what you feel and desire: you make mental space for the other person, your client. You can finally focus your complete attention on them and listen, for real.

Most people—especially salespeople—are terrible listeners. You're distracted by thoughts of the spat you had with your kid this morning, or the never-ending list of things you need to get done. If your mind is actually on the conversation at hand, it's busy predicting what the other person will say next, or preparing your response. It's focused on how *you* can steer the conversation toward the goal *you* have in mind. At the first opportunity, you jump in to finish their sentence for them, answer a question, or express your viewpoint.

There's virtually no actual listening—as in, receiving and comprehending someone else's speech—happening at all.

I used to be guilty of this too. I spent years developing scripts that were designed to lead a prospect or client neatly to the conclusion the agent wanted them to come to. Needless to say, the agent did most of the talking.

In fact, you were probably taught to believe that your value as an agent is in what you say: providing information, giving advice, and solving problems. So, you jump at the chance to speak because that's how you help your clients.

Except it's not.

On the contrary, it's impossible for you to help them until they trust you, and you build trust by *listening*, not talking. I'm not talking about some kind of fake "active listening" where you tell yourself to make eye contact, nod along, and say "I hear you" before launching into your own monologue. I mean real listening, the kind that only happens when you let go of what you want and focus exclusively on the other person.

We call that **proactive listening**—focusing *all* your attention on the other person, with the goal of seeing the world through their eyes. It's proactive in that you're watching for signs of negative emotions, and listening for ways to articulate your understanding of how they see the world. When you listen like that, you may very well make eye contact and nod along, but it's not about those outward signs—it's about what's going on in your mind. Who are you thinking about, you or them? Are you climbing aboard their train of thought, or stuck on your own? Are you seeking to make them understand, or make them feel understood?

Tool: Proactive listening

Focus all your attention on the other person, with the goal of seeing the world through their eyes and expressing that understanding.

The way you listen has much more impact on your prospects and clients than anything you say or do. Think about that for a moment. It goes against everything you think you know, doesn't it? But when you start to truly listen well, you'll see it's true.

Two-millimeter Shift: Talking → Listening

Talking is for chasing and convincing. Listening is for building trust. The way you listen has much more impact than anything you say or do.

Listen...then process...then speak to confirm your understanding.

When you do speak, instead of responding with your views, use the Tactical Empathy tools you've already learned. Label, mirror, paraphrase—all these tools require you to listen first, and keep your attention on the other person. Mirror their words to see if they have more to say about an idea. Use a label to confirm your understanding and make them feel heard. Use a deliberate mislabel to get a clearer picture of what they're really thinking and feeling.

Most importantly, if you hear yourself explaining, STOP.

As Ronald Reagan said, "If you're explaining, you're losing."

How often in a sales situation do you feel the need to explain or defend yourself? Why?

Explaining is the opposite of listening. It's a sign that you're focused on you again, and you don't build trust by focusing on yourself. It's also what you do when you're trying to convince someone of something, and remember, you're here to *find out* what's on their mind, not change it. They're not open to your influence until they trust you—until you make them feel understood.

BEND THEIR REALITY

I know what you're thinking...but what if you need to change their mind? What if they're about to make a decision they'll regret because they aren't seeing something clearly?

First of all, tread carefully here. You are not the authority on what your client wants or what is good for them. They are. Your role is not to help them decide what they want—it's only to provide enough information for them to do that themselves. Please take all your superhero capes and put them back in the closet where they belong. You don't need to save anyone from themselves. That is not your job as a real estate professional.

Remember the analogy about standing on the opposite side of the road from your client? First, you have to cross to their side and stand shoulder to shoulder with them. Then, you look at what they're seeing and where they want to go. Finally, you help them navigate the path to their destination.

In that process, there are moments when you, as an expert on the local neighborhood, will have information your client doesn't. Maybe they want to go to the top of a mountain off in the distance, but have no idea of the danger, time, or cost involved. Or maybe they want to cross to the other side of a field, but they don't know there's a marsh in the middle, and it would be easier to go around the field instead of straight through.

Let's stick with that analogy for a moment. Imagine your client wants to go to the top of a huge mountain off in the distance. They're thinking of the stunning view they'll have from up there, and if you suggest that it would be much easier and almost as good to climb a nearby hill instead, all they will see is the loss: a nice view instead of a magnificent one. Not an attractive proposition.

What they don't know (and you do) is that to get up that mountain, they'll have to cross a desert, then climb a rock face, then hike through knee-deep snow in gale-force winds. It will be dangerous, expensive, and take weeks. On the other hand, they can walk up that local hill in an afternoon.

You can't change their mind—only they can. And because fear of loss is the primary motivator of human beings (see Chapter 1), they'll do that if they perceive their previous choice as a greater loss than some other option. In this case, the client was focused on the loss of that magnificent view...but you can bring to their attention the loss of time and money and possibly life it would take to get it. Then, they can decide which loss is worse.

Chris calls this a **focused comparison**. You're not changing the facts of reality. You're just changing how the other person perceives them—*bending* their reality, if you will.

This happens all the time with home pricing. Sellers are notorious for having inflated views of the value of their homes, and they often have their hearts set on an asking price that will prevent the house from selling quickly. When you suggest they lower the price, all they perceive is the loss (of money they never had in the first place, but it doesn't matter —it still feels like a loss). What they're not thinking about is the loss of time when the house goes unsold for six months, or how much more they might have to reduce the price by that point.

> ## Tool: Focused comparison
>
> Framing the facts to focus the other person's attention on the potential losses associated with each option they face. Comparing potential losses instead of gains often changes how they think about the decision.

You can't change their mind. You can't *convince* them to lower the price, and to try would only undermine their trust in you. The only thing you can do is bend their reality. Give them a full, accurate picture of the potential losses they face with each option...and let them choose.

For example, here are several different ways to phrase the situation.

On the one hand, you want to make sure you are not going to leave any money on the table. On the other hand, you want to make sure your home sells. What pricing strategy makes more sense to you: pricing the home so the buyer is looking at what they love about the home, or pricing it so the buyer is looking at what they don't like?

Or:

You obviously want to sell your home for the most money possible. What do you think is the better pricing strategy: making the buyers reach for your price, or creating a bidding war where buyers are competing against each other for your home?

Or:

You have a number in your head that makes sense to you. Anything less would feel like a loss. The question is, what is the best way to get the result you want without jeopardizing the sale because you listed the home at a price that scared potential buyers away?

Or:

Here is what you are up against if you price your home at that number... As crazy as it sounds given this hot market, while it is almost impossible to price a home too low, it is still very possible to price a home too high. That doesn't make much sense, does it? What concerns, if any, do you have about overpricing your home so that it sits and doesn't sell...causing you to miss out on this market altogether?

Once again, it's not about you. You're here to find out what your client really wants, and help them get it. Your feelings and desires have no place in that process, and they'll only get in your way.

HOW YOU DO BUSINESS

At first glance, it's hard to believe that letting go of your desires will help you achieve them. How on earth are you going to get more clients and more income if you *stop* trying to get them? It sounds crazy.

But here's the reality I've seen over and over in this industry: when agents do things the typical way, more business brings more stress. More money and status, maybe, but also worse quality of life, and less time to enjoy that money.

There's a reason agents have a terrible reputation. They allow themselves to be defined by their production level, so they turn into mercenaries chasing after blood money. They become addicted to more, which just creates higher expectations and more pressure in a never-ending, vicious cycle.

There's a high cost to doing business that way. Just like in my first five games with the Miami Dolphins, constantly pushing for what you want actually gets in the way of doing what it takes to get it. By focusing on your goals, you push away the people who will help you achieve them: your clients.

So, forget about convincing anybody of your value, or of anything else, for that matter. The only thing you need to do is build a trusting relationship...and the only way to do that is to detach from the outcome. Let go of your feelings and desires. Focus on making them feel truly understood, and everything else will fall into place.

Your primary job as a real estate agent is to cultivate relationships on a daily basis.

I want to repeat this in capital letters: YOUR PRIMARY JOB AS A REAL ESTATE AGENT IS TO CULTIVATE RELATIONSHIPS!

The consequences of this decision will ripple through your entire business and life. It starts with the Favorite or the Fool—that concept alone saves you countless hours of pitching to people who were never going to hire you in the first place. Now, when you build trust with your clients, every conversation, every hurdle, every decision is easier to navigate. It takes less time, feels better, and occupies less of your mental space. Your clients see you as a trusted advisor, and are more likely to follow your guidance and bring you more business in the future.

Trust doesn't just give you more time and money—it brings you joy and inner peace.

That's what we mean when we say that how you do business is more important than how much business you do.

This is what happens when you do business as an authentic human being with other human beings. You're not a commodity, and they're not paychecks. We're all here on earth to be of service to others, and you're learning how to find the people who want your help...and help them.

KEY TAKEAWAYS

→ Explaining value is about fact, logic, and reason. Building trust is about emotion, connection, and relationships.

→ The first one seems easier, but it doesn't work because that's not how people really make decisions. Plus, it turns you into a commodity, because there's always someone who will promise more and charge less.

→ When you take the time to build trust first, everything that follows will be better and easier.

→ The key to building trust is letting go of your feelings and desires. That's what allows you to focus your complete attention on them, and truly listen.

→ You can't convince anyone to do anything, and to try only undermines their trust in you. Instead, influence them by bending their reality, i.e., focusing their attention on potential losses they hadn't previously considered. Then, preserve the trusting relationship by letting them make the decision.

Tactical Empathy Toolbox

→ **Proactive Listening:** Focus all your attention on the other person, with the goal of seeing the world through their eyes.

- **Focused Comparison:** Framing the facts to focus the other person's attention on the potential losses associated with each option they face. Comparing potential losses instead of gains often changes how they think about the decision.

Chapter 4

GET THE ELEPHANTS
OUT EARLY

||||||||||||||||||||||||||||||||||||||||||||||||||||||||||||||||||||||||||||||||||||||||||||||||||||||||||||||||||||

*The reasons someone might **not** want to do
business with you are more important
than the reasons they do.*

||||||||||||||||||||||||||||||||||||||||||||||||||||||||||||||||||||||||||||||||||||||||||||||||||||||||||||||||||||

AFTER NURTURING A POTENTIAL CLIENT FOR OVER FIVE YEARS, Tracey* finally got the listing. The owner, Dave*[9], was ready and motivated to sell, and Tracey would have been elated, but there was just one problem: Dave's expectations were unrealistic.

He wanted to list at $1.5 million without doing any staging, and he was convinced that his market research justified that price. Tracey knew better, and she gently suggested that the price might be a little high, and that staging was probably a good idea, but Dave wasn't interested. She

---

[9] Names have been changed.

figured she could either take the listing on his terms or lose it, and she wasn't about to give up on a prospect she had put so much effort into already.

So, they did what he wanted and waited to see who would bite... and waited, and waited some more. Weeks went by with no offers. No one even wanted to come see the house. It was clear that Dave's plan had been a bad idea.

Now, Tracey is in a tough spot. She can try to convince Dave to lower the price by $100K and invest $10K in staging, and if she succeeds, the house will probably sell quickly. That won't feel like a win to Dave, though. He'll think he lost $110K, and because a loss stings twice as much as an equivalent gain, he'll *feel* like he lost $220K. That's not the kind of emotion that leads to referrals.

If she fails to convince him, or if she doesn't try, the listing will expire. Another agent will come in, relist at a lower price, and get the commission, while Tracey walks away with nothing to show for all her effort.

She's between a rock and a hard place, and it's all because she didn't get the elephants out early.

She's not alone—the vast majority of agents do exactly what she did, and you probably do too. My coaching calls are full of problems just like this one: tough conversations that agents dread to have with their clients.

Pricing is a common sticking point, but it's far from the only one. Tough conversations happen throughout the process, from getting hired all the way to closing the deal. Anytime your client's desires and expectations don't match up with reality, you've got a tough conversation on your hands.

Depending on how you approach them, these conversations can build one of two things: trust or resentment. Unfortunately, our instincts tend to lead us down the second path instead of the first.

In this chapter, you'll learn why the usual way of addressing problems is so counterproductive, and how to do it in a way that strengthens your relationship with your clients instead of undermining it. Instead of treating tough conversations as threats, you'll see them as opportunities.

THE OLD WAY:
AVOID AND SUGARCOAT

No one likes to be the bearer of bad news. Bad news upsets people, and you don't want your clients to be upset—you want them to be happy. You want them to have confidence in you. You want them to *like* you.

Telling them something they don't want to hear doesn't seem like the best way to achieve that, does it? If you reveal the ugly truth, you might lose the client or the deal.

So, you try not to mention anything that might drive them away. When you're wooing them to hire you, you focus on why they should work with you, and avoid any hint of why they might not want to. That includes your commission—ideally, it never comes up until they see the contract, and then they just sign without questioning it, and you breathe a big sigh of relief.

When you're getting ready to list (or search for properties, if your client is a buyer), you prefer not to crush their dreams, even if you know their expectations are totally out of whack. They'll figure it out for themselves when they see that their house doesn't sell, or their budget won't get them everything they're hoping for. That way, reality is the one that disappoints them, not you.

Some ugly truths can't be avoided, though. When the inspection reveals problems, when the counteroffer gets rejected, when the other side is asking for concessions...you have to say something.

If you are like most agents, you dread these conversations. They're the ones that keep you up at night, imagining how your clients will explode at you, or maybe even fire you. It's the absolute worst part of your job, so you often find yourself delaying and searching for ways out of the situation. Standard practice is to take the problem, stick it in a drawer, and hope it goes away magically.

How much time have you spent spinning things in your head in an effort to preserve what you hope is the client's favorable opinion of you?

At some point in the transaction, though, you have to face the music. When that time comes, you play down the negatives and look for a silver lining or some kind of solution to the problem, hoping that might mitigate their anger and disappointment. As the saying goes, "Bring me solutions, not problems." If you do that, they can't fault you, right?

Whether you're avoiding or sugarcoating, minimizing your client's negative emotions is the name of the game.

I get it. If you're anything like most agents, you're a people person... dare I say, a people pleaser. You hate to upset anyone, and you hate even more for anyone to be upset *at you*. You know unhappy clients won't refer to you in the future, and they make you miserable in the present, so you do everything in your power to squash negativity.

Unfortunately, while avoiding and sugarcoating may seem to keep negative emotions at bay, what those tactics really do is generate stress and undermine your clients' trust in you. People may not like hearing bad news, but what they like even less is getting blindsided by it, and that's exactly what happens when you try to tiptoe around the tough stuff. When they finally see the problem, they think, *Why am I hearing this now when you could have told me ages ago?*

There are only two answers to that, and neither one makes you look good. The first is you didn't anticipate this problem, in which case your competence comes into question. The second is you did anticipate it, but didn't say anything, which makes them wonder what else you're holding back, and whose interests you're prioritizing—theirs or your own. The cover up is always worse than the crime.

Instead of protecting your relationship with your clients, avoiding and sugarcoating bad news has inadvertently wrecked it.

THE NEW WAY: BE A STRAIGHT SHOOTER

Bad news is a bummer, but you know what everyone likes? A straight shooter: someone who tells it like it is, and doesn't keep you guessing or try to pull the wool over your eyes.

Instead of shying away from problems, a straight shooter confronts them head-on as soon as they become apparent, just like the buffalo in the storm. While this may seem scary, it always leads to better outcomes for both you and your client. If the problem is a dealbreaker for them, it's better to get it on the table now than to waste more of anyone's time on a deal that will never close. If it's not, they'll thank you for bringing it up as soon as possible.

Don't mistake this transparency for brutal honesty. We're in the business of making people feel understood, and brutality has no place there. There's no reason honesty has to feel like a brick to the face, and it never should if you're delivering it right.

That's what the rest of this chapter is about: how to deliver bad news and confront negative emotions in a way that makes people feel understood. You'll learn exactly what to say, how to say it, and why these nuances of language are such powerful tools for building trust with your clients.

CALL OUT THE NEGATIVES

If you've been in an airport or on public transit recently, you've probably seen signs that say, "If you see something, say something." That's a Department of Homeland Security slogan urging you to report suspicious activity to law enforcement, but you might as well print that out and slap it on your office wall, because it applies to real estate too.

In fact, it applies to every kind of tough conversation, from family spats to hostage negotiations. It's one of the key negotiation tactics that Chris learned in his time with the FBI, and continues to use with all his negotiation coaching clients. Only instead of reporting suspicious activity, you're calling out negative emotions.

Whenever you sense that your client is unhappy, say so. It doesn't matter whether you know the reason why. It doesn't even matter if your interpretation of their mood is correct. If you see something, say something: "You seem upset/frustrated/disappointed," or whatever emotion fits best.

You probably think this sounds crazy. Why would you call attention to a negative emotion—isn't that just inviting it out to play? And what if you're just imagining it—wouldn't that just create a problem where there wasn't one?

Here's the truth: it's *impossible* to speak a problem into existence. If you're mistaken, they'll correct you, no harm done. If you're not, and there really are negative emotions happening, naming them actually reduces them.

That's science. Studies have shown that when people label their negative emotions, their physiological experience of those emotions diminishes.[10] All those stress symptoms that pop up when you're upset—elevated heart rate, shallow breathing, high blood pressure, sweating, nausea, muscle tension, etc.—actually get better when you put a label on what you're feeling. (Remember labels from Chapter 2? Yep, here they come again.)

Why does this work? It all comes back to Tactical Empathy, a.k.a. making people feel understood.

When someone tells you not to feel something (*Don't be upset!*), does that make you feel understood? Of course not. It does the opposite —it convinces you that they don't understand your perspective at all. Denying negative emotions has a 100 percent failure rate.

---

[10] Alex Korb, *The Upward Spiral: Using Neuroscience to Reverse the Course of Depression, One Small Change at a Time* (Oakland: New Harbinger Publications, 2015).

What about when they ignore what you're feeling? No, you don't feel understood then either. Once in a while, unspoken negative emotions just fade away, but most of the time, they fester like an untreated wound. Not pleasant.

You're probably starting to see why labeling negative emotions is the way to go. By calling them out instead of waiting for the other person to bring it up, you show that you're paying attention to how they feel. When they feel understood, their brains release oxytocin, which mitigates the stress response. Your label doesn't fan the flames of negativity—it douses them.

This works even if the label is completely wrong. If you say, "You seem upset," when they're not, they won't hesitate to say, "No, I'm just thinking through my options," or whatever else is going on in their heads. As we mentioned in Chapter 2, a mislabel often leads the other person to reveal even more information than a correct label does. And it still makes them feel understood, because you've shown your consideration for their feelings, and given them an opportunity to communicate their thinking.

GET IN FRONT OF THINGS

The fear of speaking problems to life also keeps agents from preparing their clients for what lies ahead. Before you ever talk to a prospective client, you already know about all the objections they might have to working with you, not to mention all the obstacles they might face once the work begins. But if you're like most agents, you don't say anything. You just cross your fingers, and hope those issues won't come up.

That automatically puts you behind the ball. It sets you up for that ugly question: *Why didn't you tell me sooner?* Don't put yourself in that position. Instead, bring up those objections and obstacles before they take you down.

Once again, this might seem crazy. Why on earth would you talk about reasons not to work with you when your goal is to convince them to hire you? Why would you freak them out now about problems that may or may not come up during the sales process?

Because it builds trust.

Two-millimeter Shift:
Waiting ➜ Getting in Front of Things

When you delay the delivery of potentially negative information, you undermine the other person's trust in you. Instead, bring it up as soon as you can. If it's a dealbreaker, you waste less time, and if not, your transparency builds trust.

Not long ago, Chris was shopping for a new car. At the dealership, he asked the salesman if the chassis of the car he was looking at was good. "Of course!" the salesman said. "It's the best on the market!"

Would you have believed that guy? Yeah, neither did Chris.

THE FULL FEE AGENT

Now, imagine the salesman had said something like, "Well, it's the best on the market for off-roading, but it's not the most comfortable for city driving and long road trips."

Suddenly, he seems like a trustworthy source of guidance for your car purchase. And look at how he did it—by anticipating a possible objection. Instead of pretending his product was perfect, he acknowledged up front that it wasn't ideal for everyone.

Could that cost him a sale? You might think so, but think again.

Would anyone who objected to a stiff ride have ever bought that car anyway? No, but they might have wasted another hour of the salesman's time before figuring out the car didn't meet their needs. Or worse, they might have bought the car and then brought it back a week later, having realized their mistake. Either way, the salesman would have been better off if the customer had walked away in the beginning.

That's why the reasons someone might *not* want to do business with you are more important than the reasons they do. You are not a trustworthy authority on your own value...unless you also acknowledge the client's potential objections. Then, instead of convincing the client to hire you, you're simply informing them and allowing them to choose for themselves. As we mentioned in Chapter 1, people will die over their autonomy. When you let them keep it, their trust in you grows.

Two-millimeter Shift:
Why ➔ Why Not

The reasons someone might *not* want to do business with you are more important than the reasons they do.

Warning people about potential obstacles achieves the same thing. Just imagine your friend invites you to go for a walk in the park. Only when you arrive do you realize that it's a National Park, and the trail is several miles of hilly terrain. You're totally unprepared, and by the end, you're exhausted, dirty, sunburnt, bug-eaten, and dehydrated. Oh yeah, and angry at your friend.

Now, imagine that instead, she invites you on a long, challenging hike and advises you to wear sturdy shoes and bring water, sunscreen, bug spray, and a raincoat, just in case. It's the same trail as before, but in this scenario, you're ready for it. It's still a tough hike, but at the end, you're grateful for the advice she gave you, and happy you didn't even need to use the raincoat.

Preparing your clients for the possible challenges ahead won't scare them off—if it does, they weren't ready for this road anyway, and working with them was never going to end well. For the clients that *are* ready, discussing potential issues before they arise can only build their confidence in you. It shows you know what you're doing and want them to have the best possible experience. If any of those problems come to pass, they'll be thankful for the advance warning, and if nothing bad happens, they'll be even happier that you were able to smooth the road for them.

BRACE THEM FOR BAD NEWS

In this business, there's no escaping bad news. No matter how well you do your job, problems happen. Sometimes they're outside your control, and sometimes they're not. Sometimes you anticipated them and warned your client, and sometimes you didn't. Regardless, you have to deliver the message.

The good news is that people want you to tell them the truth... gently. Don't just blurt it out, but don't dance around it either. Instead, ease them into it with two powerful techniques: bracing and the Accusations Audit.

Bracing is deceptively simple: "I have some bad news."

Those five words give you the ability to have any tough conversation. They instantly make it easier for both you and your client to broach any uncomfortable subject.

Tool: Bracing for Bad News

Before you deliver potentially negative information, prepare the other person by saying, "I have some bad news."

This is one of the most important and valuable phrases you will learn in this book. "I have some bad news..." is such an incredibly versatile turn of words, and can be used in so many different situations. Once you get comfortable with this language, you will never fear another difficult conversation. It gives you a way in whenever there is something challenging that needs to be discussed.

These words inspire dread, which is, unbelievably, the point. When you say them to a client or prospect or agent, the first place their mind goes is death—literally.

Bad news? What could it possibly be? In a fraction of a second, they're already picturing the most horrifying thing they can think of.

That's the beauty of it: the actual bad news is almost never as bad as they imagined. Instead of going from neutral to upset, they're going from terrified to upset, which actually feels like a *relief.* The facts of the situation are no different, but they feel less terrible than they would have if you hadn't braced them.

Two-millimeter Shift:
Sugarcoating ➜ Bracing

When you try to put a positive spin on bad news, it comes across as disingenuous and manipulative. Bracing them for it softens the blow.

There's a second reason this works so well. The regions of the brain that react to emotional pain are the same as those for physical pain, and studies of physical pain show that bracing for it can actually reduce the perceived intensity of the pain. If you say, "This is gonna hurt," the person prepares mentally, and if the blow strikes within a short window after that, it hurts less than if it had struck without warning. You can't wait too long, though, or the anticipation itself becomes painful.

So warn them, wait for them to give you permission to proceed, then let it fly. This concept is one of the easiest things to implement in this whole book, and it instantly transforms your approach to tough conversations.

DO AN ACCUSATIONS AUDIT

You can take this even further—and we strongly recommend that you do—with an **Accusations Audit**. When you anticipate that a client (or anyone else) will have a very negative reaction to your news, this is an essential tool for reducing the fallout.

The essence of it is this: before you deliver the bad news, you tell your client all the horrible things they'll think and feel when they hear it. You lay out all the possible accusations they might make, no holds barred (which is why it's called an Accusations Audit). You keep going with the accusations until the client pushes back, and *only then* do you deliver the news.

Tool: Accusations Audit

To defuse potential negative emotions, articulate all the awful things the other person might think or feel in response to your message.

The easiest way to understand this is to see it in action. So, let's go back to the story of Tracey and Dave from the beginning of the chapter. Tracey has to tell Dave that the house won't sell unless he lowers the price and invests in staging. If she's savvy enough to use bracing and the Accusations Audit, here's how that conversation would go.

Tracey: "Dave, I have some bad news."

That's bracing. She's asking permission to deliver the truth.

Dave: "Uh oh. What's going on?"

She just got the go-ahead signal.

Tracey: "You're not going to want to hear this. You're going to be furious. You'll think I have no idea what I'm doing. You might even want to fire me."

With these accusations, Dave starts to wonder what could possibly be so bad.

Dave: "What do you mean?"

Tracey: "You're going to wonder why I didn't say this before. You'll probably question my intentions, and think I deceived you in some way."

The more extreme the accusation, the more Dave wants to distance himself from it. He wants to think of himself as a reasonable person, not someone who would think or say those things.

Dave: "I wouldn't think that, Tracey."

He pushes back on the accusations, giving Tracey the signal that it's safe to deliver her message.

Tracey: "The reality is, this house won't sell unless we get it professionally staged and lower the price by $100K."

She delivers the news clearly, without sugarcoating, apologizing, taking responsibility for the situation, or trying to solve it. She simply states the facts, then waits in complete and total silence.

Dave: "Wow. Okay. I appreciate your honesty. That's a tough pill to swallow, but I guess we have to do what we have to do. Let me think about it overnight, and I will get back to you in the morning."

The next day, Dave might come back and say, "My wife and I talked this over. We've got to be realistic about this if we want it to sell. Let's do it. Lower the price and let's set up the staging."

What just happened? Why wasn't Dave upset after Tracey told him exactly what he didn't want to hear?

It's the same thing that happens with "I have some bad news," only more powerful. If you overblow the prospect of negativity, when you finally deliver the news, it feels like a relief. By verbalizing your client's worst possible reactions ahead of time, you actually inoculate against them. You take away their gunpowder.

It's simple, but counterintuitive. Put yourself in Dave's shoes. You like to think of yourself as a reasonable person, not someone who would explode with rage. You chose Tracey to help you, and don't want to think you put your trust in the wrong person. So, when she says, "You're going to want to fire me" and "You're going to think I deceived you," your instinct is to distance yourself from that. By saying those things, she made you want to *avoid* making them true.

Two-millimeter Shift: Solving Problems ➜ Defusing Negative Emotions

When problems come up, your instinct is to solve them, but that's not what your clients need. Instead, use an accusations audit to defuse their negative emotions so *they* can make an informed decision about how to proceed.

Notice that Tracey *kept going* with the accusations until Dave pushed back on them. That was the signal that he didn't want to think and feel those things, and had braced himself against them. At that point, he had decided to receive the news calmly, no matter how bad it was. That's when Tracey knew it was safe to proceed.

This pushback can manifest in different ways. Here are some of the things clients might say that signal they're ready to hear your message:

- I wouldn't think/say/do/feel that.
- You're being too hard on yourself.
- It can't be that bad.
- Just tell me already.
- Rip the bandaid off.

The more trust you've built with a client, the quicker this happens. When trust is weak, it can take a lot more accusations to get to this point. If their verbal or body language (including silence) in any way indicates they might agree with your accusations, you haven't gone far enough yet.

That's why it's important to prepare thoroughly for the conversation. Before you go into this situation, sit down and write out all the negative things the client could possibly think or feel in response to what you're going to tell them. Be specific. For example:

- You're going to be crushed/furious/disgusted/etc.
- You'll probably feel that I let you down.
- You're going to think I should have seen this coming.
- You'll probably wonder how this could happen when the market is so hot.
- You're going to think I was out of touch with the market.
- You'll probably think I'm only concerned about my own interests.
- You'll probably want to fire me on the spot.
- You'll think I'm the worst agent in the world.
- You're going to hate me.

Remember, it's impossible for a label to plant a negative thought that wasn't already there, so get as extreme as possible. There's no way to overdo it. The harsher the negative label is, the more likely your client will push back on it, which is exactly what you want.

As you prepare, you can also use the same strategy to reduce your own negative emotions. Just label all the negative things you're thinking and feeling as you anticipate the conversation. For example:

- I'm feeling fearful.
- I'm afraid the client will yell at me.
- I'm looking for a way to sugarcoat this.
- I'm looking for a way out of this conversation.
- I'm scared.

Another thing you should do to prepare is practice your **late night FM DJ voice**. Slow down and speak in a low, soothing tone, as if you were the host of a late night radio show. This tone is highly effective at getting other people to relax and slow down because calm is contagious.

Tool: Late Night FM DJ Voice

A low, slow, soothing tone of voice that's highly effective at getting other people to relax and slow down.

Look back at Tracey and Dave's conversation. At any point, did she explain her thinking, defend herself, or debate with her client? No. She just laid out what she imagined Dave would be thinking and feeling, then delivered the truth. That's all you need to do. You don't need to solve the problem, or even explain how it happened. You just need to deliver the news gently, and that's exactly what the Accusations Audit allows you to do. It minimizes the negativity that both you *and* your client experience.

Sometimes, you don't get the chance to do an Accusations Audit before the bad news drops. Instead, your client finds out first, and then you have to deal with the aftermath. The Accusations Audit is still useful in that situation. All you have to do is adjust your phrasing: "You'll probably _____" becomes "You probably _____," and "You're going to _____" becomes "I know you _____."

Here's an insider tip from Chris: "I know" is the way to go when the other person is really upset. He started using "I know" instead of "You probably" when talking to the families of kidnapping victims. Imagine saying to the parents, "You're probably worried about your daughter's safety." *Probably?* It's insulting just to imply there might be a chance they're not. But you're not guessing—you *know* they're worried. So, say so.

SILENCE IS YOUR FRIEND

Once you've delivered the news, there's one more thing you need to do: shut up.

Seriously. Just stop talking. Let there be **silence**. Don't try to fill it —the other person needs it. They need mental space to process what you've just said and consider their options, and if you keep speaking, you're stealing that from them.

Most people can't stand silence in a conversation. They think it means something is wrong, so it makes them feel extremely uncomfortable. The reflex is to fill it with anything you can think of—small talk, platitudes, questions, anything to keep it from being awkward.

But what if silence actually means something *good* is happening? What if it's an indicator that the other person is doing exactly what you need them to do: *thinking* about what you've just told them?

Tool: Silence

After you deliver your information, stop talking. Give the other person ample space to process what you've said and express themselves. Let them break the silence. It's not awkward— it's essential.

If you're like most agents, when you deliver bad news, or lay out a tough choice for your clients, you usually jump straight into problem solving. Instead of stepping back and giving the client room to think, you try to do the thinking for them, and it's not out of the goodness of your heart. It's out of fear. Maybe if you can solve the problem, the client won't get upset or blame you for it.

But your problem solving is just getting in their way. How well would *you* think with someone jabbering at you nonstop?

Silence isn't just something you should learn to tolerate. It's a tool you need to use proactively in every tough conversation you have. Do your Accusations Audit, deliver the bad news, and be quiet. The last step is just as important as the first two.

In the next chapter, you'll see exactly why.

KEY TAKEAWAYS

→ When you avoid tough conversations and sugarcoat bad news, you undermine your clients' trust in you, and their ability to make informed decisions.

→ Everyone likes a straight shooter—someone who tells the truth *gently*.

→ Don't beat around the bush or try to solve the problem for them. Just brace them for the bad news, and use an Accusations Audit to defuse their negative emotions.

→ Once you've delivered the news, be quiet. Silence gives the other person the space they need to process what you've said and consider their options.

Tactical Empathy Toolbox

→ **Bracing for Bad News:** Before you deliver potentially negative information, prepare the other person by saying "I have some bad news."

→ **Accusations Audit:** To defuse potential negative emotions, articulate all the awful things the other person might think or feel in response to your message.

→ **Late Night FM DJ Voice:** A low, slow, soothing tone of voice that's highly effective at getting other people to relax and slow down.

→ **Silence:** After you deliver your information, stop talking. Give the other person ample space to process what you've said and express themselves. Let them break the silence. It's not awkward—it's essential.

Chapter 5

PUT THE RESPONSIBILITY WHERE IT BELONGS

Own your role as the trusted advisor.
It's not your job to decide anything—
only your client can do that.

ONE OF MY COACHING CLIENTS, VICTORIA*, HAD A FRIEND, JASMINE*[11], who wanted to help her purchase a multimillion-dollar home. Jasmine wanted to work with someone she trusted, so she reached out to Victoria, who was thrilled at the prospect of working with her friend. While Jasmine's expectations seemed a little unrealistic, Victoria agreed to help her because she didn't want to disappoint her friend. You've all been in a similar situation.

---

[11] Names have been changed.

Unfortunately, Victoria's instincts were right. After several months of looking and writing offers and missing out on properties, both Victoria and Jasmine were feeling exhausted and frustrated, and there was some unspoken tension building between them. Victoria was disheartened because she felt like she was letting Jasmine down. In her mind she was responsible for getting Jasmine into a new home, and she was failing. This client relationship, which she had thought would be fun and easy, had actually created a massive amount of unnecessary work and anxiety in Victoria's life.

Don't blame the client, though. The agent is the one at fault here, but not for failing to get her friend into a new home. Her problem was strictly in her own head.

She was taking on responsibility for things that were outside her control.

She didn't control what her friend was willing to offer for a new home. The only thing under her control was making sure Jasmine saw the best properties and knew what it would take to complete a successful purchase, including price, terms, contingencies, timing, etc. She had no ability to make Jasmine pay more than what she wanted.

Victoria was putting herself through the emotional grinder day after day for something that wasn't her responsibility at all. Real estate agents do this to themselves all the time, and not just when the client is a friend. You think you should control every aspect of the process, so when something goes wrong, you think you're at fault—or if not at fault, at least responsible for solving the problem.

Here's the hard truth: you have no decision power in this process.

Your role is to be an advisor. It's not your job to decide anything—only your client can do that. All you can do is lay out the landscape and present their options. You can make recommendations, but you can't make them do anything. If you've built enough trust in your relationship, you can influence them (as you learned in Chapter 3), but you can't force their hand.

Most agents don't understand this, so they make themselves crazy and end up taking the blame for everything that doesn't go their way. Stop it. It's worse than unnecessary. It's burning you out, wrecking your client relationships, and getting in the way of actually solving problems. I can't tell you how many times I've listened to agents torturing themselves and beating themselves up for things that were never in their control. It's a very bad habit that agents need to address if they're going to have any level of sanity in their lives.

In this chapter, you'll learn to own your role as the trusted advisor. Once again, it comes down to detaching yourself from the outcome—leaving your feelings, desires, and need for control behind so your client can make the decisions that are rightfully theirs. It will take a huge weight off your shoulders, moving you one step closer to feeling truly joyful and at peace in your work.

THE OLD WAY: TRY TO SOLVE EVERYTHING

If you're like most agents, you never made a conscious decision to try to solve every problem and make every decision in the sales process.

You just have this gut feeling that you *need* to. When a problem or choice comes up, your instinct is to tackle it, and you never think twice about whether it's yours to tackle.

It feels like an instinct because it comes from a very old emotion: fear. You're afraid of what the outcome of the process will be if you don't dictate every move.

Agents get so attached to the outcome in part because they sell their services on the basis of promises about that outcome. When you overpromise to win a client, then you feel responsible for fulfilling the promise. At a conscious level, you're afraid that if you don't, they'll walk away, or if they stick it out, they'll be unhappy with the result and bad-mouth you. Unconsciously, your brain is taking that train of thought to its "logical" conclusion: if you lose your clients, your business will fail, you'll go broke, end up on the streets, and *die*.

Thus, the fear...but none of that is real.

We've been through this before—you won't die. On the contrary, if you stop grasping for control and detach yourself from the outcome, you'll actually get out of your own way, just as you did in Chapter 3.

Think of all the things you take responsibility for that you have no real control over. If you're like the agents we coach, the list is long: pricing, staging, when to list, when to hold open houses, choosing a buyer, making offers and counteroffers, accepting or rejecting offers, handling inspection issues...and all the other miscellaneous problems that pop up in every deal.

You don't have the final say in any of this, but you try to convince, or even make decisions for, your clients anyway. After all, they hired you for your expertise, so you know what's best. They'll appreciate you taking the lead as the expert, right?

Not so much. In fact, not at all. Not even a little bit.

Never forget: people will die over their autonomy (see Chapter 1). When you take decisions away from them, or push them to choose, they resent you for it. You know this—just think about the last time you felt pressured to make a choice. Did you like that? Of course not. Neither do your clients, or anyone else.

Plus, taking responsibility for everything makes your life miserable. Anxiety and guilt pile up when things don't go perfectly, which is usually. You blame yourself, and the client does too, because when you took on responsibility, they gave it up. Everyone ends up in a negative emotional state, and the relationship starts to unravel.

THE NEW WAY: ADVISE AND GUIDE

Let's go back one more time to how you and your clients start out on opposite sides of the street. Instead of yelling at them to come over to your side, first you need to cross to their side and stand shoulder to shoulder with them. Then, you have to look at the view from their perspective and see where they wanted to go.

Now comes the next step: gently guiding them to their destination.

Taking responsibility that isn't yours is like grabbing them by the wrist and dragging them up the road. Even if you're taking them where they want to go, they don't want to go like that.

THE FULL FEE AGENT

Instead, just point out the possible paths, let them choose, and walk by their side to be there when they need more guidance. That's the only way to preserve their autonomy, which is a crucial element in building trust, cultivating influence, and making the experience positive for them regardless of where they end up. If they feel in control, they're more likely to feel satisfied with the final outcome, and even if they don't, they won't blame you.

You are not responsible for the outcome—you are accountable for doing what you say you are going to do. Your job is to lay out the landscape as best as possible. The client has to choose what direction they want to go.

> ### Two-millimeter Shift:
> ### Responsibility ➜ Accountability
>
> You are not responsible for the outcome—you are accountable for doing what you say you are going to do. Your only job is to give your client the information they need to make their own decisions with confidence.

Remember, the only things you really have control over are how you market the listing (on the sell side) or how you search for listings (on the buy side), and how you conduct yourself with other agents. Everything else is beyond your power. It's all up to the client, and you can only educate and guide them.

IT MATTERS WHO SAYS IT

Let's say you have a client who insisted on an inflated asking price and, as a result, hasn't received any offers. I bet this has happened to you before, so if you can recall a specific instance with a real client, think about that situation for a moment. Remember how you felt and how they felt after months of crickets from the market.

Now, imagine this: you say to your client, "We need to cut the price by 10 percent."

How do you feel as you're saying it? Probably some combination of anxious, frustrated, apologetic, and exhausted. You *need* them to agree, or the listing will expire without selling, and all this work will have been for nothing.

How does the client feel? Not too jazzed either, I'm sure. You said before that the house could sell at this price, and they had their heart set on it. Now, all they see is a 10 percent loss, and it was your idea, so it's on you.

Okay, now back up. What if, instead, *your client* said to *you*, "We need to cut the price by 10 percent."

That's a totally different ballgame. Instead of being at loggerheads, suddenly you're collaborating. They might not be thrilled to cut the price, but they're doing it willingly to get what they really want: a sold house. They understand that trade-off and have chosen to make it of their own free well, without pressure or coercion. You, needless to say, are massively relieved and happy to help them execute the decision they've made.

It's the same idea as the first scenario, even the exact same words, but it came out of your client's mouth instead of yours. That's what we mean when we say it matters who says it.

When it comes to guiding and influencing your clients, think about it this way: whatever you want them to do, they need to think it's their idea. At the very least, they need to feel it was 100 percent their choice to pursue that idea.

Two-millimeter Shift:
Leading ➔ Guiding

Taking the lead in the decision making process violates your client's autonomy. Instead, provide the information they need to navigate the decision while letting them stay in the driver's seat.

How would Victoria get Jasmine to say they need to cut the price by 10 percent? By playing the role of the trusted advisor. Remember, advisors don't make decisions, and they don't tell their clients what they need to do. They don't *need* to do anything, and you can't make them. All the advisor does is lay out the options and the likely consequences of each one.

So, she might say something like this, in her most deferential and respectful tone of voice: "With the house priced at $5 million, we haven't received any offers in over two months. If you keep that asking price, the house could remain unsold for six months or more. If you reduce the price to $4.5 million, we're likely to find a buyer within a couple of weeks, possibly multiple buyers. How would you like to proceed?"

First, she stated the facts of the situation. Then, she laid out the alternatives, stating them clearly as the *client's* choices. Obviously, Victoria favors one option over the other, but instead of saying so, she just emphasized the loss the client would experience if she didn't choose that option: the house would *remain unsold*. (That's bending reality, from Chapter 3.)

Finally, she put the ball squarely in Jasmine's court by asking her to own the choice. Not pressuring her to choose or suggesting which choice would be best—just giving her the space to consider the options, with her autonomy fully intact.

NOTHING IS PERSONAL

One of the greatest dangers of taking on responsibilities that aren't yours is that you'll feel that you can't bring up a problem until you have a solution. Agents feel that if they're delivering bad news, they have to fix it—they can't just let the client sit with it and make the decisions about how to deal with it. So, they don't get the elephants out early like they should.

When you do this, your mind isn't on the client's needs—it's on you. More specifically, it's on your fear of how the client will respond to you. Because you don't want the client mad at you, you don't share what the client needs to know to make an intelligent decision. You put them at a disadvantage to protect your own ego.

But it's not about you. *Nothing in this business is ever about you.*

I said it in Chapter 3, and again in Chapter 4, and I'll say it one more time now: your emotions and desires have no place here. (Spoiler alert: I'll probably say it again before the book is done.)

How you feel is irrelevant, but for so many agents, that dictates how they behave. Plus, when your vision is clouded by your emotions, you can't read your clients, and you certainly can't make them feel understood. How can they feel understood when all your attention is on you?

When an issue comes up and you start to have feelings about it—whether that's anxiety, frustration, anger, hope, or anything else—the first step is to recognize that you're having thoughts and emotions about this. Label them, just like you do when you're preparing an Accusations Audit. Then, acknowledge what's driving them: your fear of what will happen if you don't control the process.

Remind yourself that you are not in control. You cannot decide, only advise. You're not here to steer the process, only to find out where it will go. When you detach from the outcome, you can finally become the trusted advisor your client wants and needs.

Your feelings hold you back from that, so just let them go. Breathe, meditate, calm yourself down in whatever way works for you. I promise it gets easier with practice.

EMPATHY, NOT SYMPATHY

Like any new, learned behavior, it's normal to struggle with it or feel some resistance. One common source of resistance is the cultural idea that you help someone else by feeling their pain. Emotions are contagious—that's just human nature. When we see people smiling, we smile. When we see people get upset, we get upset. Just put a few babies together and wait: when one of them cries, the others start crying too.

But there's a reason we call it Tactical Empathy and not tactical sympathy. Are the other crying babies helping the first baby by sharing its emotional experience? Nope. That's sympathy, and it's natural, but not very useful in this situation. You feeling upset on your client's behalf is equally ineffective.

Tactical Empathy is the art of articulating what someone else is thinking and feeling, *without* necessarily agreeing or feeling the same way. That not only makes them feel understood, but it also prevents a disastrous feedback cycle of negative emotions between the two of you. Not only do you not need to feel bad about their problem (and remember, it is *their* problem), but you can be much more helpful if you don't.

If you stay calm and detached from the outcome, you can just lay out the facts and the options, then let them sit with the information until they're ready to make a decision.

I'll end this chapter with a real life example of an agent who had to put the responsibility where it belonged in a big way to move forward with a client. The agent had been working with the seller for four months already, preparing the house for sale. The price was originally going to be $3.95 million, which made sense for the market at that time. The agent wanted the seller to do $30,000 of work to get the house market ready, and the seller was reluctant but agreed.

THE FULL FEE AGENT

Then, three weeks before going on the market, the agent spoke to a trusted colleague who worked in the area, and his fellow agent thought the price was closer to $3.5 million. All of a sudden, panic took over. *What if the price really is $3.5 million? What if I just had my seller spend $30,000 on staging that they wouldn't have spent if they knew the price was only $3.5 million? How am I going to explain this? What are they going to think of me? What if I don't tell them? What if I just wait to see how the market responds to the higher price?*

The agent did *not* want to have this conversation with the seller. He worried and berated himself for days, imagining what the client would say and trying to find a solution before he had to break the news. The emotional agony made those days miserable, even when he wasn't actively working at all.

But look at what he was taking responsibility for: the movements of the market and the seller's asking price. He didn't control either of those things, and he couldn't solve this problem. He could only educate the seller about the new reality, and allow him to decide how to proceed.

The agent didn't need a solution, and he didn't need all that angst either. All he needed was to detach from the outcome, put the responsibility where it belonged, and get the elephants out early (complete with an Accusations Audit).

In the end, the agent figured out that $3.95 million was actually the right price. The property was listed at that price and sold quickly at full asking. All of this back and forth and mental anguish was totally unnecessary. Even if the price had needed to be lowered to $3.5 million, it was always going to be the seller's decision. What the client needed was simply a clear picture of the options, and the autonomy to make the choice that was best for him. Would he have been happy if he had to lower the price by $500,000? Of course not. But instead of feeling blindsided by the situation and manipulated into a decision, he would have appreciated the agent's transparency and professionalism. That's the power of being a trusted advisor.

KEY TAKEAWAYS

→ Agents habitually take responsibility for problems and decisions that aren't theirs, which causes huge amounts of unnecessary stress and work.

→ You don't own any of the decisions in this process. Only your client can make them, and when you try to do that for them, it violates their autonomy.

→ You can only advise and guide them. Your only job is to provide the information they need to make a decision with confidence.

→ When they decide for themselves—even if you guide them— they will be more committed to their choice and collaborative in implementing it with your help.

→ It's not helpful for you to get upset about problems on their behalf. You can understand their feelings without sharing them, and you're better equipped to guide them from a place of calm than a place of stress.

Chapter 6

LET THEM SAY NO

People hate to say yes, but
they love to say no.

You've probably heard of momentum selling. It's that decades-old strategy where the salesperson asks a prospect a series of questions, all of which are designed to elicit a yes answer. Even if you've never heard the phrase "momentum selling," you've definitely had it done to you by a telemarketer or sidewalk fundraiser.

For example, here's a classic listing presentation technique taught by a leading real estate trainer:

Agent: Do you absolutely have to sell your home?
Prospect: Yes.
Agent: Do you want to get top dollar?
Prospect: Yes.
Agent: Do you want me to handle the sale?

119

Prospect: Yes.

Allegedly, it's that simple.

From the salesperson's perspective, momentum selling is an attractive idea. All you have to do is ask the right series of questions, and people will feel like they *have* to say yes to your offer. It makes sense on the surface: people don't like to contradict themselves, especially not in an obvious, public way, right? So, if you get them to say yes to easy, non-committal questions, they'll be more likely to say yes to an offer that's aligned with those answers.

The rule of thumb is that if a person says yes three times, you've succeeded—you'll get a sale. Each yes is a tie down, and by the time you've got three, most people won't be able to escape.

If you're wondering whether that's as sleazy and manipulative as it sounds, the answer is yes.

Buyers *hate* this tactic. Why do you think people hang up on telemarketers and avoid eye contact with sidewalk fundraisers? They know what's coming, and they don't want to get trapped. When they do get caught in a momentum selling ambush, they might say yes, but their actions probably won't support their words.

So, why do so many salespeople (including real estate agents) still do it? Well, it *seems* to work. At least, it can bring your closing rate to something more like 5–10 percent. For someone whose closing rate was close to zero, that could be a tenfold increase! You can't argue with that, can you?

Well, we're gonna.

If you've been paying attention, you knew that already. This way of selling goes against everything you've learned so far. If you're only pursuing opportunities where you're the Favorite, your closing rate should be closer to 100 percent than 10, and you don't need underhanded tactics to achieve that because those prospects chose you before you ever met them. And if you're building a business on trust instead of value, undermining your clients' autonomy by trapping them into saying yes is a surefire way to fail.

Salespeople are obsessed with yes. Even if they're not using momentum selling in this stereotypically slimy way, they're looking for other ways to get to that magic word. Every yes is a victory.

Not for clients, though. What feels like a win to you feels like vulnerability to them. When they say yes, it's usually with caution, wariness, and skepticism. That emotional state is not at all conducive to building a trusting relationship where they enjoy working with you and are open to your influence. You want your clients to feel safe and in control, not vulnerable and guarded.

So instead of *yes*, you're going to aim for *no*.

That probably sounds crazy. In business, yes means progress, and no means getting stalled. How can it possibly be productive to aim for no?

In this chapter, you'll find out.

THE OLD WAY: PUSH FOR YES

For a moment, think like a regular person, not a salesperson. When someone approaches you with an offer or request, what's your first instinct? If you had to give a yes or no response within half a second, before you've had time to think about it, what would you say?

No. Every single time, no.

When you walk into a store and the salesperson immediately asks if they can help you find anything, you say no, even if you *are* looking for something specific.

When a stranger calls and asks if it's a good time to talk, you say no, even if you're not busy.

When your teenage kid asks to borrow the car, you say no, even if there's no good reason.

No is safe. It's the status quo. When you're not sure if something will be good for you, you protect yourself by pushing it away. Even when you do end up saying yes after you consider the situation, your very first instinct was to say no.

That's why salespeople try to use questions that couldn't possibly have any answer other than yes. *Do you want to make more money? Do you care about children? Could you spare a dime a day?* If you say no, you feel like a liar, an idiot, or a jerk.

It can be more subtle too. Back in the day (before I met Chris), I wrote tons of sales scripts designed to lead people down a very reasonable, logical path to yes. *Do you want to net the most money possible? Do you want a strong negotiator representing you? Do you want to make sure you're not leaving any money on the table?*

Like I said before, that stuff works. At least, it works better than *not* doing it...if you're trying to sell your value to every person that walks in your door.

Those sales scripts do get people to agree, and salespeople celebrate every yes they get, but they shouldn't. Those victories are hollow, and liable to disappear at any moment.

Think about it—when you get pressured into saying yes to a question that couldn't possibly have any other answer, you're suspicious. What does this person want from you, and how are you going to keep them from manipulating you? So you say yes, but it's not real. You're just leading them on to find out what else they're going to say...and how you can get out of this conversation gracefully.

That's what you're doing to your clients when you use momentum selling. They'll say yes to make you happy and get you off their back, but they probably don't mean it. In the meantime, you've undermined their trust in you by threatening their autonomy. Next time you talk, they'll approach the conversation with resistance ready to go in advance.

We don't want rejection, so why do we keep doing things that invite it?

It's like a slot machine. Most of the time, you strike out. But every once in a while, you win one, and it feels so good that you forget all the losses. So, you keep pulling, even though that thing is going to bankrupt you eventually.

It's time to kick the yes habit.

THE NEW WAY: MASTER NO

People hate to say yes, but they love to say no. Once they've said no, they're actually more open to listening to you because they've protected themselves and established their control over the situation. Their autonomy is intact, and you aren't threatening it, so they actually have the mental space to process what you're saying.

So, start by triggering a no on purpose. Instead of asking questions designed to lead to yes, ask questions where a no serves you, a.k.a. a **no-oriented question**. For example:

- *Would you be opposed* to me sharing a story?
- *Would it be unreasonable* to do a Zoom call before I visit the property?
- *Would it be impossible* to stage the property before we list it?
- *Are you totally against* the idea of us working together?
- *Would it be wrong* to assume you've formed an impression of whether you want to work with me?
- *Would it be crazy* to think you have a price in mind?
- *Would it be out of line* to ask if you're considering other agents?
- *Would it be off base* to say you're looking to sell quickly?

You can take the beginnings of those sentences and finish them with whatever you want—whatever would make a no work in your favor. You're not restricted to that formula, though. Any yes-oriented question can be turned around into a no-oriented question or statement.

> ## Tool: No-Oriented Question
>
> A question designed to elicit a no response, where no moves the conversation forward instead of shutting it down.

For example, shop salespeople usually ask, "Can I help you find anything?" If they really want to help you (maybe they work on commission), they should say, "You probably know what you're looking for and don't need my help."

Here's a common one: when you call people, you probably ask, "Is now a good time to talk?" Instead, you should ask, "Is now a bad time to talk?"

They could say, "Yes, it's a bad time, I'm very busy," but they usually don't. Why? *Because people love to say no.* It's not a logical thing—it's emotional. No matter which question you ask, the first thing they want to say is no. So, ask the question where no moves the conversation forward.

You'll see this for yourself when you try it with your prospects. You know sellers expect agents to come give a listing presentation, and you also now know that this free consulting is killing your business. It's not necessary, or a good use of your time, and you want to avoid doing it.

Here's how you use a no-oriented question to achieve that: *Would you be opposed to doing a video call before I come out to the house?*

They almost always say no.

Turn it into a yes-oriented question (*Could we do a video call before I come out to the house?*), and you'll get a very different response: resistance. *Why do we need to do that? Why is this person asking something unexpected of me?* They want to say no, and with this yes-oriented question, no is unhelpful.

No-oriented questions unlock all kinds of barriers. When people feel safe, they'll listen more openly, offer information more freely, and collaborate more readily.

CALIBRATED QUESTIONS™ [12]

The key to all that information and collaboration is calibrated questions. These are open-ended questions that are calibrated to put the other person in an open frame of mind towards you. Usually, they're how or what questions. For example:

- What would need to happen...?
- What would that look like?
- What criteria are most important to you?
- What should the next step be?
- How should we proceed?
- How will you decide?
- How would you see us working together?

---

[12] One of the Black Swan Method Negotiation 9 Skills. More in-depth training on the Negotiation 9 is available at www.blackswanltd.com.

With these questions, you're showing deference to the other person, which warms them to you. People love to be asked what they think. It makes them feel respected, valued, and heard.

Tool: Calibrated Questions

Open-ended questions (almost always beginning with how or what) designed to put the other person in an open frame of mind towards you.

You're also prompting them to think deeply. This stops people in their tracks, and forces them to carefully consider whatever situation or choice you've put in front of them. Instead of dwelling on their emotional reaction to it, they focus on solving the problem or clarifying their desires and intentions, within the safety of their own autonomy.

That's why these questions are so effective at revealing important information and inviting collaboration with your clients. As you learned in Chapter 5: whatever you want them to do, they need to think it's their idea.

Before you can break out the how and what questions, first make them feel understood. Use mirrors and labels to get them to say "that's right" (flip back to Chapter 2 for a refresher on this). You'll feel that emotional click when you get in alignment with them, and that's when you can start guiding them to where they want to go.

How and what questions put the ball in the other person's court and make them think. Their answers reveal what they will and won't do, so you don't have to guess. Here are some examples of calibrated questions that can work in many situations throughout the real estate sales process:

- What are you really hoping for?
- What is important to you about that?
- What would make this a great experience for you?
- What is most important to you during this process?
- What are your biggest concerns?
- What are you basing that on?
- What have I left out?
- What else do we need to discuss?
- What happens if...?
- What would need to happen...?
- How would you like me to do that?
- How long do you want to try that?
- How will you know...?
- How do you see that happening?
- How do you want to handle this?
- How are you going to decide?
- How do you see this playing out?
- How are you going to feel if...?
- How have you done this in the past?
- How do you like to...?

DON'T TAKE THE BAIT

This chapter has been all about asking questions. That's how you focus on the other person—it's standing shoulder to shoulder and seeing what they're seeing. It's a huge part of the trust-building process.

But, as you already know, salespeople like to answer questions, not ask them. You've been trained that your value is in having all the answers. You think: *If I don't have the answer, why would anyone work with me?*

So, you jump to answer questions because it's a chance to demonstrate your value...especially when they ask, "What do you think?" That's your favorite one.

Don't take the bait!

Your clients don't want to know what you think. They only want to know if you think what they think. They already have something in mind, but they're just not ready to commit to it quite yet.

The real question is, *why* do they want to know what you think? This is the moment to find out. What's the thought that's already in their mind, and what are their feelings around it? If they're not confident in their decision yet, where is that uncertainty coming from? What are they afraid of, and what other information do they need to move forward?

Labels and calibrated questions will help you find out. Tailor them to the situation—start with a phrase like "It seems like you have doubts about..." or "What would you need to know to decide..." and fill in the specifics. Keep going until you have a clear understanding of why they're stuck.

That's how you help them get unstuck—not by simply making a recommendation but by digging down to the root of the issue and solving it at that level.

In the end, it's always on you to put the ball back in their court: "If it were me, this is what I would do...But it's not me, it's you, and it's your decision to make. How do you want to proceed?"

KEY TAKEAWAYS

→ As a salesperson, you're trained to get to yes, and it feels great when you do. But for the customer, saying yes makes them feel vulnerable and wary.

→ What people really want to say is no because it feels safe. No preserves the status quo and protects their autonomy.

→ So, begin with no-oriented questions. Once they've said no, they'll be more open to your guidance.

→ Then, use calibrated questions to prompt them to think deeply and share their thoughts with you.

→ If they ask what you think, don't take the question at face value. Dig deeper to uncover what they're already thinking, and why they feel uncertain about it.

Tactical Empathy Toolbox

→ **No-Oriented Questions:** Questions designed to elicit a no response, where no moves the conversation forward instead of shutting it down.

→ **Calibrated Questions:** Open-ended questions (usually beginning with how or what) designed to put the other person in an open frame of mind towards you.

Chapter 7

NAIL THE LASTING IMPRESSION

*Send people away in a limo, and there's
a good chance they'll come back.*

IMAGINE YOU'RE REPRESENTING A SELLER AT THE END OF A DEAL. You've got an offer from a serious buyer, you got the inspection done, and you've spent a week going back and forth, trying to get both parties to a place where they can agree. You've resolved every negotiation point and are only $3,000 apart on price.

So, you do what most agents would do: you split the difference. The seller and the buyer each eat $1,500. It's a simple, fair solution, right? Your client doesn't love it, but you convince them it's the only surefire way to close the deal. They agree to it because you've invested weeks into this process now, and the last thing they want is to relist and start again from scratch.

Finally, the deal is done. It only took two months from the time the seller contacted you. They wanted to sell quickly, so you see that as a huge win. Plus, they got almost their full asking price and only had to make a few repairs. You think they should be thrilled— thrilled enough to work with you again in the future, or send referrals your way.

But they're not. They don't say anything negative to your face, but they just don't seem as ecstatic as you thought they'd be. You never hear from them again, and they never send anyone your way. What happened?

You didn't think about the last impression. Everyone tells you to worry about first impressions because you only get one chance. Sure, but usually there's at least a little time to recover if it doesn't go well.

Not so with the last impression. That's the feeling that sticks, and because it's last, you really don't get another chance. And for a business built on repeat and referral customers—as yours should be—you can't afford to neglect the last impression.

In this story, everything went smoothly until the end of the deal. But what stuck in the client's mind was that last concession, the one they were reluctant to make, but felt like they had to. It wasn't even a lot of money in the grand scheme of things, but it felt bad, like the buyer got something they shouldn't have, and you couldn't prevent it. The seller got almost everything they wanted, but that sour taste from the end of the negotiation is what they'll remember.

This happens *all the time,* and most of the time you don't even know it. In this industry, 90 percent of buyers and sellers say they would work with the same agent again, but only 20 percent ever actually do. Yikes.

At the very beginning of this book, I showed you why repeat and referral business has to be the foundation of your work. It's the only way to run a successful real estate business that allows you to actually enjoy your life. It's a natural consequence of doing business as a human being instead of a commodity.

In this chapter, you'll learn how to make sure your lasting impression is the kind that will bring people back for more.

THE OLD WAY: EVERY CLOSED DEAL IS A WIN

Agents love closing deals. It's what puts money in their pocket and sends their production numbers up. It's what they brag about. It's what they live for.

For an agent, every closed deal brings a massive sigh of relief. There's always the chance that all your hard work could come to nothing at the last minute. When it doesn't, that's cause for celebration. You assume that your clients feel the same way.

They might...but they might not. It's not about how close the deal ended up being to what they originally wanted. That would be logical, but as you already know, there's way more going on in the human mind than just logic.

It's about the quality of the emotional experience they had in getting to the deal, especially at the end. Did they feel like they were fully informed and in control of their decisions, or like they were roped into things they weren't really okay with? Did they feel like they made the right trade-offs to get what really mattered to them, or like they gave up more than they should have? Do they feel you protected their interests and helped them make the right decisions, or you just wanted to get the deal done?

That's what really matters.

So no, every closed deal is not a win. It's only a win if the client *feels* like they won. It doesn't matter what the deal looks like on paper—only their emotional experience of it. Your goal isn't to close the deal. It's to make sure they walk away happy, regardless of the business outcome.

THE NEW WAY:
FOLLOW THE OPRAH RULE

The last impression is the lasting impression—Chris knew this intuitively from his hostage negotiation work, but he first heard it articulated and verified at a Gallup conference in 2008. You know Gallup, the company that does all those polls you hear about in the news. They had a mountain of data about human behavior and how people recall past events, and the evidence was right there.

People don't remember how it happened. They remember the most intense moment and how it ended.

That explained why Chris and his FBI teammates had been able to get the upper hand in multiple hostage situations just by taking control of the *end* of each conversation with the kidnappers. If the kidnapper had a habit of hanging up with no warning or putting the call on hold, the FBI team focused on getting him to finish the conversation properly: say goodbye and hang up. That's civilized and respectful behavior, and it completely changed the emotions and balance of power in the negotiation.

After the conference, Chris talked about the idea of the lasting impression with his friend Cindy Mori, who was Oprah's booker at the time. "Of course," she said. In most of the entertainment industry, you come in a limo and leave in a taxi. Not with Oprah. On her show, you come in a limo and leave in a limo, literally and figuratively.

Of the thousands of people who went on that show over twenty-five years, who comes to mind who has bad-mouthed Oprah? There were never any serious public spats or feuds, and any rumors along those lines disappeared quickly because her guests only ever had nice things to say about their experiences. People loved how it felt to go on Oprah as much as they loved to watch it, which is why she was able to get so many famous and powerful people to come back again and again.

That's what you're aiming for. Send people away in a limo, and there's a good chance they'll come back.

This doesn't just apply to clients who close deals with you. It applies to *everyone*, no matter the circumstances under which they walk away from you. That includes prospects who decide not to work with you, and clients who decide to let their listings expire unsold or switch to another agent. It also includes other people who work with you, like the other party's agent or vendors for things like home staging and repairs.

When people walk away happy, they come back again later, ready to collaborate with you again…and that makes your life *so* much easier.

You already know that customer acquisition costs are what really kill real estate agents. All the time and money you spend finding clients eats away at your bottom line like a termite infestation. But when a customer comes back for more or sends you a referral, that business lands in your lap practically for free. You need as much of that as you can get.

Plus, it's much more productive and enjoyable to work with someone who already has a positive relationship with you, or at least a positive impression. Without that, they're likely to be skeptical and guarded, which means you have to build trust from the ground up. It's doable, as you've learned, but it takes time. Working within an existing trusting relationship is that much more efficient.

So, how are you going to make sure everyone walks away happy?

NEVER SPLIT THE DIFFERENCE™

Chris called his first book *Never Split the Difference* for good reason: everyone does it all the time, and it's always a bad idea.

Real estate agents are the guiltiest of all. Splitting the difference is the default solution to every negotiation problem. We see it all the time—every single one of my coaching clients reacts with shock and confusion when they learn they need to stop doing it. Most of the time, they have no idea what else to do.

You probably think Chris and I are crazy. What could be more fair and reasonable than a fifty-fifty compromise?

But compromise is never equal.

Let's go back to the story from the beginning of the chapter. When the seller agreed to split the $3,000 difference with the buyer, what really happened in their head?

Well, you learned in Chapter 1 that the pain of a loss is twice as powerful as the pleasure of an equivalent gain. So, that $1,500 loss *felt* like $3,000, whereas the other side only gave up half that. In theory, for your client to feel like the split was fair, they would give up just $1,000 while the other party ate $2,000. Splitting the difference down the middle is *never* going to feel good for your client.

When agents can't split the difference—or don't want to ask their client for another concession—they usually have one backup plan: chip in and cover the cost themselves. Agents are notorious for reaching in their own pockets to make a deal come together. You believe something is better than nothing, so to avoid losing the whole commission, you just sacrifice a little chunk of it.

You think you're securing your business by chipping in, but in reality, you're undermining it.

This is a sign that your business is based on explaining value, not building trust. Without trust, the only value you can offer that means anything to them is your time and money. So, to get as much out of you as possible, they treat you like a bank. Whenever they need your time or money to move the deal forward, they feel entitled to it. After all, that's effectively what you promised.

You think you're getting emotional bonus points for your generosity, but you're not. You're just setting the expectation that it's okay for your clients to reach into your pocket. Plus, you're confirming to them that your time is an unlimited free commodity and your money is cheap. What they perceive is that you can't even make a deal come together without opening your own wallet.

In a trust-based business, the client doesn't ask you to chip in. If you've built a strong relationship as their trusted advisor and consistently put the responsibility where it belongs, why would they? They understand that you're here to educate, support, and protect them—not to pay their bills. They're not looking for a discount because they know you're worth every penny, and they wouldn't want to disrespect you by implying that you don't deserve your fee.

When the transaction is the only thing that matters, you'll give things away to get it done. When the relationship is what matters most, you recognize that it's not healthy for one party to feel entitled to stick their hand in the other's pocket.

So, if you want your clients to feel like they're riding away in a limo, you can't split the difference, and you can't just chip in to make the problem go away. You've got to do something different.

I don't mean some kind of special negotiation tactic or closing trick. In fact, you've already learned exactly what to do.

MAKE THEM FEEL UNDERSTOOD

That's it: practice Tactical Empathy. Make them feel understood.

You did this at the beginning of the relationship, when you were finding out if you were the Favorite or the Fool. You did it when you were building trust, breaking bad news, and guiding them to make informed decisions. You need to keep doing it until the very end—*especially* at the very end.

The end of a deal process is a test of your commitment to Tactical Empathy. As you get closer and closer, you'll be more and more tempted to default to your old salesperson habits. You'll get impatient and start looking for the first opportunity to close, pushing everyone else, including your client, to get there faster. The fear will creep in, and bait you into throwing Tactical Empathy to the wind. This is why you often feel like no good deed goes unpunished.

Don't give up.

Go back to what you've learned in this book. When you detach yourself from the outcome, you get out of your own way. Just give your best effort as an authentic human being who is here to serve others, and the results will take care of themselves.

How you behave at this stage should be no different from what you've done up to this point. First, you prepare for every conversation by thinking through (and ideally writing down) what everyone else is likely to be thinking and feeling.

For example, here are some things a potential seller might be thinking, in no specific order:

- Should I sell?
- What is my house worth?
- Will I get the price I want?
- Is now the right time to move?
- Does it make sense for me to sell my house in the current market?

- How much money will I net?
- What are closing costs?
- What other costs are associated with selling?
- What does the selling process look like?
- How much time will it take to sell my house?
- How involved do I have to be in this process?
- Will the process be stressful?
- What agents should I interview?
- Do I really need an agent?
- Can I sell the house myself?
- What is a standard commission for an agent?
- Will I have to hold open houses?
- What will my neighbors think?
- Am I making the right decision?
- Where will I move to?
- Where do I begin?
- How do I feel about this?
- Will this be difficult?
- How do I go about finding the right agent?
- Why are different agents giving me conflicting information?
- Why are agents telling me a different number than Zillow?
- Should I put money into updating my home?
- Can I sell my home as is?
- What will buyers think of my home?
- Are buyers going to ask for credits or repairs?
- Will I be sad to leave this home?

NAIL THE LASTING IMPRESSION

- How much work do I have to do?
- What if the house doesn't sell?

Examine what you're thinking and feeling as well, and recognize that your thoughts and feelings have no place here and won't help you. Let them go.

Then, during the conversation, you listen with your full attention to the other person. Use mirroring, labeling, and mislabeling to elicit more information and make them feel heard. Aim to get to "that's right." When you feel that click of emotional alignment, you'll know they feel understood.

That's when you can start guiding them to where they want to go. Lay out the landscape for them: the facts of the present situation, the options they have, and the likely consequences of each option. Then, use calibrated questions to make them think about (and reveal to you) what they truly want and don't want. Only they can decide what to do, so give them the space to do that with a simple question: *How would you like to proceed?*

Don't fall into the trap of thinking your role as the expert is to tell them what to do. Even if they act like that's what they want, it's not. They're just scared—this is a big decision, probably the biggest financial transaction of their life, and they don't want to screw it up.

That doesn't mean they actually want you to decide for them. They just want to feel empowered to make a decision with confidence.

The key to that isn't giving your opinion or recommendation. It's showing them the full decision landscape, and being transparent about the inherent uncertainties involved. Even you, the expert, can't say 100 percent for sure what the consequences of any given decision will be. You can share your best educated guess, and be honest about your level of certainty around it.

Give them all the information you would consider if you were making the decision for yourself...but don't make it. That's their job. When you do that, they will feel supported and in charge of their own destiny.

At no point in time do you try to convince them of anything. Be patient. You're not here to *make* something happen with fact, logic, and reason. You're here to explore the unknown and *find out* what will happen.

LIMOS FOR EVERYONE

That's what makes people walk away with a positive emotional experience of interacting with you. It even works when they decide *not* to work with you.

For example, let's say you're talking to a prospect, and they've got their heart set on an inflated asking price. You strongly believe the house won't sell at that price point, and you know it would be a waste of time and bad for the client relationship to accept the listing at that price, only to have to reduce it later.

So, you use the same process. First, you listen with your full attention and make them feel understood. Then you lay out the situation: your view is that the market won't support that asking price, and you wouldn't want to waste the seller's time pretending that it does.

It seems like you are committed to listing your home at $X or above. You've probably spoken to an agent who feels confident they can get you that price. Unfortunately, I see the market differently. You deserve to work with someone who believes in your price.

If the seller wants to go with someone else, that's okay! It's their prerogative. Send them away in a limo anyway with this offer: *If for any reason things don't work out, and you feel I can help you, please feel free to reach out and contact me.*

You made them feel understood, allowed them to make an empowered decision, and ended on a positive note. When their listing expires with that other agent, they'll be back.

KEY TAKEAWAYS

→ The last impression is the lasting impression. If a deal closes in a way that doesn't feel good to the client, that negative emotion is what they'll remember.

→ That's a huge problem for your business. People who walk away unhappy won't work with you again, or refer others to you.

→ Follow the Oprah Rule: send everyone away in a limo. That means practicing Tactical Empathy in every relationship, all the way to the end.

→ Splitting the difference and chipping in to make a deal come together are lazy tactics that undermine your relationship with the client. Don't give into the temptation to use them—practice Tactical Empathy instead.

→ All of this applies to every relationship, regardless of whether the person chooses to do business with you now. If you send them away in a limo, they're more likely to come back again.

Chapter 8

BE A FULL-SERVICE, FULL FEE AGENT

At 6 percent, real estate agents are the biggest bargain on the planet.

WHEN YOU GET THE LISTING INTERVIEW PHONE CALL, IN YOUR HEAD, you are a 6 percent agent.

In your car going to the appointment, your fee is now 5.5 percent, with you keeping 3 percent.

As you get out of your car to go to the front door, your fee is now 5 percent.

When they answer the door, you blurt out unprovoked, "My fee is 4.5 percent!"

Does this sound familiar in any way?

If you want to know what it means to be a full-service, full fee agent, look no further than Regina Vannicola.

She's one of our coaching clients, and like every agent who works with us, she used to be in the habit of making herself into a doormat. She prided herself on doing whatever it took to get the listing and close the sale, and if that meant discounting her fee or caving to crazy client demands, she did it.

Virtually all agents do. It's not that they like being doormats—no one does. They're just afraid of what will happen if they don't.

After learning what you've learned in this book, Regina decided to be brave and find out. When a developer called her about listing a unit he was converting from an apartment into a condo, she went to see the property with a new mindset: Not, *What do I have to do to get this listing?* But, *Is this opportunity a good fit?*

This developer was a mover and shaker who owned lots of income properties in the community. Obviously, he was an old hand at real estate deals, and because so many agents discount their fees, Regina had doubts about whether he'd be willing to pay her full fee.

So, instead of avoiding the issue, she got the elephants out early. After touring the property, she said, "I've got some things we need to talk about that could be deal breakers for you. This is going really well, but I might throw a wrench in the works with this information, so I'd like to put it on the table now. Would you be opposed?

"No, go ahead," the developer said.

"Here's my top ten list of reasons why you won't want to work with me."

"*Ten?*" he asked.

"Well, no, there are really only about four," she said, and the developer laughed. She continued, "First and foremost, I'm a full-service, full fee agent. I charge 6 percent, keep 3.5 percent, and give 2.5 percent to the buyer's agent. I'm going to encourage you to price the property so that it will sell quickly, and that might very well be a price that's less than what you'd like to see. I'm going to encourage you to invest in preparing it for sale, and you're going to need to stage it. The last thing is that I don't work 24/7. You'll never need me and not get me, but you won't need me at 10 p.m., and my phone goes off at 6."

The developer took a step back and said, "Wow, that's a lot of conditions! We just met."

Regina laughed and said, "I actually prefer to think of them as standards."

He paused for a moment, then asked, "Why don't you split the commission equally with the buyer's agent?"

At that moment, she knew she was hired. He wasn't balking at her standards, just asking a question about a detail that wasn't an important factor in his decision. With that knowledge came an upwelling of self-worth, confidence, and power.[13]

Most agents cringe at the very thought of approaching a prospect with a list like that in the very first conversation (or any time, for that matter). But when Regina talks about doing it, she can't stop smiling.

Laying out the potential deal breakers—especially the commission —up front has saved her *massive* amounts of time and frustration. It quickly weeds out the bad clients, and the people who were never going

---

[13] Watch Regina tell this story in her own words: https://www.youtube.com/watch?v=22 DDQRIERlk.

to hire her anyway. What she's left with are clients who believe in her worth and are ready to work collaboratively.

Plus, she just doesn't have to sell as many homes to hit her income goals. Do the math: if you charge 5 percent and keep half, you have to sell *40 percent more homes* than if you charge 6 percent and keep 3.5 percent. How would your life be different if you had 40 percent more time for yourself, or 40 percent more income for the same amount of effort? A 1 percent difference might seem small, but don't be fooled—it will transform your business and life.

In this chapter, we'll tie together everything you've learned so far into the mother of all tough conversations: your standards...*especially* your commission.

You'll see that standing firmly by your fee isn't about being greedy. It's about being the best agent you can be for your clients. That might sound crazy now, especially if you're thinking there's no way you can get away with charging 6 percent in your market. By the end of this chapter, you'll see that it's not just sensible—it's imperative, for your sake and your clients'.

THE OLD WAY: DOORMAT YOURSELF

Commission is the one topic that scares agents more than anything else. Everyone has an opinion, but no one wants to talk about it with an open mind. There's a select group of agents who charge a full fee on one side of the street, and then everyone else—a much bigger group—on the other side, with virtually no middle ground. There is an overwhelming belief that you cannot charge a full fee and thrive in this business. Everyone wants to pretend there is nothing they can do about it. *It's a losing battle,* they tell themselves. *What's the point in hashing it out again?*

And yet this is probably the most important conversation that needs to happen. Commission is where the rubber meets the road in real estate. Your ego, your value, your self-worth, your self-confidence, your pocketbook, your future—it's all up for grabs in that one moment when a potential seller asks, "What is your fee?"

That's all it takes to make a real estate agent squirm. I can get a discount from ninety-nine out of one hundred agents just by asking that one, simple question. The default response to even the slightest hint of pushback on your fee is to hand out a discount, even when the client hasn't actually asked for one.

Why?

It all comes back to fear. Fear that you're not really worth 6 percent after all. Fear of being an imposter. Fear of being rejected. Fear of what will happen if you lose this opportunity.

To that, we say *stop it!* Stop letting fear run your life, and stop giving your money away!

You work too hard and too long to just let people reach into your pocket as if they were entitled to do so. Every buyer and seller wants your money. Whether they ask up front or at the end of the transaction or somewhere in between, they're going to ask. Count on it. They always have a "legitimate" reason to ask, and you always have a "legitimate" reason to give in.

But the truth is, no one ever needs your money—they just want it because they think they can get it. If someone needs your $500 or

$1,000 or $10,000 or more to buy or sell a home, they shouldn't be doing the deal.

If only agents were as protective with their commission as they are with their split with their brokerage. How do you feel when your sales manager calls you into their office and says they need to lower your split? Do you just roll over? Of course not! But when a buyer or seller does the same thing, suddenly you become shy and small and timid. It makes no sense.

Bottom line: you *can* and *must* charge 6 percent.

As Chris always says, at 6 percent, real estate agents are the biggest bargain on the planet. In any other industry, a finder's fee is 10 percent.

I've coached enough agents that I know you can charge 6 percent in any market. It doesn't matter if your competitors are charging less. It doesn't matter if you're a super high-end agent working with multimillion-dollar listings. Save your excuses—we'll get to those in a minute. First, we need to fix a false assumption that's holding you back.

THE NEW WAY: FULL SERVICE, FULL FEE

Imagine this for a moment: what if a prospect told you they didn't care about your fee? What if price just wasn't an important factor in deciding who to hire?

You would charge your full fee, of course. If you know without a doubt that they don't care, why wouldn't you?

Well, guess what? *They actually don't care.* I know this sounds insane, but just bear with me for a minute.

In one study of B2B sales, researchers broke down the sales process into nine steps, from the initial search for potential solutions all the way to engaging with a sales rep from the chosen vendor to make the purchase. Customers get pricing information in step three, but they don't reach out to vendors until step eight. In between, they're busy evaluating all their options and consulting with other people about the decision. By the time they talk to vendors, their mind is already 70–100 percent made up.

You already know this—it was one of the first things you learned in this book. When a prospect calls you, you're already the Favorite or the Fool.

Here's the crazy part. Customers know a vendor's price way back in step three. If they get all the way to step eight and contact that vendor, they've reconciled themselves to that price. Otherwise, they would have eliminated that option by then.

In fact, researchers asked what the most important factors were when evaluating vendors (step three) and making the final choice (step nine). At step three, price is the number one consideration. At step nine, it doesn't even make the top five. What they really care about is whether the solution is the right fit.

Whether it's B2B or B2C, humans are humans. If that's how they make major business purchases, it's how they make major personal purchases too, including hiring a real estate agent. They know long before they call you that 5 to 6 percent is the industry standard commission. By the time you talk to a prospect, price is *not* a major factor in their choice.

You already said it: if you knew a prospect didn't care about price, you would charge your full fee.

So from now on, that's what you're going to do.

ARE YOU THE FAVORITE?

Here's the real secret to getting a full fee. It's not about providing more value, being more persuasive, or changing anyone's mind. (You know by now that none of that has any place in your business anymore.)

It's a function of one thing only: are you the Favorite or the Fool?

If you're the Favorite, they'll pay your full fee. They might ask questions or push back a little, but they'll pay it in the end.

If you're the Fool, it doesn't matter what your fee is—they're most likely not going to hire you. If you chase every low-probability deal and keep handing out discounts, sure, you might convert some of those prospects. But at what cost?

Discounting is a hard habit to break. If you do it once, you'll do it again, and it can become a crutch very easily. That has long-term ramifications for your business that most agents never consider.

Here's an exercise that will make you sick to your stomach: go back to your first day in real estate and add up all the money you've given up by discounting or chipping in. Go on, do it. The total number will shock you.

You may think you never would have gotten some of that business if you hadn't discounted. Maybe, but you have no idea how much *more* business you would have done without those discount clients getting in the way.

As you learned back in Chapter 2, having to convince someone to work with you is a bad sign for the relationship. Those are the worst clients—skeptical, untrusting, and demanding—and one bad client takes up the space of two good clients. In other words, one discount client takes up the space of two full fee clients. If you've been operating under the illusion that discounting is good for your business, it's time to face reality.

Let's go back to something else from the very beginning of the book: you can't overcome emotion with fact, logic, and reason.

This statement is at the heart of every commission discussion. Sellers don't want to feel foolish by paying more than necessary—*feel* being the operative word here. You've probably studied all kinds of commission dialogues that try to convince people with facts, logic, and reason that you're worth what you charge...but you can't overcome emotion with facts, logic, and reason. There's no convincing anyone to feel less foolish.

People will pay you 6 percent because they *feel* they absolutely want to work with you. In every interaction, you've demonstrated qualities—like trustworthiness, competency, and transparency—that give that person confidence in your abilities. They know you're going to do what you say, and put their interests first at all times. They don't want to go through this process without you.

All because you made them *feel understood*.

Those are the clients you want. With them, you're the Favorite. They will gladly pay your full fee, collaborate with you, be open to your influence, and appreciate your hard work.

To make room for them, you have to walk away from everyone else. Make 6 percent your standard, and stick to it fearlessly. You're not afraid to have the commission conversation, and you're not afraid to say "no thank you" to those who aren't willing to pay 6 percent.

It's that simple. I've studied this from every angle possible, and the ability to charge 6 percent is not a function of market conditions, geography, list price, experience, or production. It depends on just this: do you have walk away power?

If you're not willing to walk away from anyone who won't pay you your full fee, you won't be successful charging 6 percent. End of story. Six percent needs to be a standard.

And as Clayton Christensen, a former Harvard Business School professor, said: it's easier to do something 100 percent of the time than 98 percent of the time.

From now on, you charge everyone 6 percent, no matter the situation or circumstance. If a seller can't accept your fee, that's okay—you just walk away.

Seriously, no exceptions. Just imagine a handful of your best clients getting together by some chance. The conversation comes around to you and what you charge. How would that conversation go? Would you be getting irate phone calls because you were charging different amounts to different people? How would that affect their trust in you and willingness to refer business to you or hire you again in the future?

Making 6 percent your standard is better for your business in so many ways...and it's also good for your clients. Charging a full fee forces you to become a better agent because to charge more, you have to provide exceptional value. To provide more value, you have to examine every aspect in your business: your mindset, strategy, prospecting, follow up, marketing, showing, negotiating, problem solving, and everything in between. Does it all align with a 6 percent fee?

In *The Science Of Getting Rich* by Wallace D. Wattles, the author says: "Give every person more in use value than you take from them in cash value. Then you are adding to the life of the world with every business transaction."

Challenge yourself to live up to your 6 percent fee. The irony is, you'll end up doing more business and making more money by becoming more conscious about the work you do, and the value people derive from it. At first, insisting on 6 percent sounds greedy and selfish, but the reality is the exact opposite: it keeps you on your toes, and inspires you to do your very best work at every opportunity.

NO MORE EXCUSES

I know all the reasons why you feel you must lower your fee. *All of them.*

No matter what your excuse (and it is an excuse), the underlying reason is fear. You think there is not enough business out there for you. If you don't discount, you'll lose to someone else who will, and something is better than nothing. Time after time, you convince yourself there is no other option other than to concede. It's just the cost of doing business.

It's all B.S. The pull in this industry to discount is so strong, and there is such a herd mentality when it comes to your fee. So, let's address the most common excuses directly.

Excuse #1: Discounting has always worked for me.

You've gotten this far, right? Why fix what's not broken? You've been discounting practically since day one, and you're convinced that it's a key reason for your success so far.

Chris likes to compare this to teenage boys shaving. At some point, every boy hears that shaving makes your facial hair grow faster and thicker. This isn't actually true, but they don't know it. So, the second a hair appears, they whip out the razor and have at it. Sure enough, they start to see more and more facial hair.

But that hair growing had nothing to do with the shaving. It was going to grow anyway, razor or no razor.

You think discounting is the reason you've won business...but is it? How do you know? Even if your clients said they'd go with someone else unless you reduce your fee, how can you be sure they weren't bluffing?

You can't. You also can't know what other business you might have won if you had let those discount clients walk.

You've already heard all the ways discounting is hurting your business without you even realizing it. So yeah, it's broken, and yeah, you do need to fix it.

Excuse #2: No one will go for that—all the other agents charge less.

Over and over, agents tell me: *Six percent can't be done. No one in this market is doing that.*

The second part might be true, but that doesn't make the first part true.

In Chris's early days as an FBI hostage negotiator, no one ever asked the kidnappers to put the hostage on the phone. It couldn't be done, they said. When asked, the kidnappers always refused. It made getting proof of life (evidence that the hostage was, in fact, alive and in custody) extremely difficult.

But what if they asked in a different way? "Can I speak to the hostage?" was a yes-oriented question, and it wasn't working...but maybe a calibrated question would change the game. So, they tried it: "How do we know the hostage is alive?"

It worked. All it took was a little tweak in their approach, and something that couldn't be done suddenly became an extremely effective standard protocol.

We hear this excuse from most agents, but top performers and luxury agents are the biggest offenders. They fool themselves into thinking it's all about market share. More signs means more sales.

I don't disagree that more signs means more sales, but I do disagree with giving your money away to get more signs. If you're losing market share over commission, there's something else at play that you don't want to address. It's just easier to lower your fee than to closely examine the value you provide.

Anyone can give their money away. There is no skill or special talent in lowering your fee from 6 percent to 5 percent or 4 percent or lower. It's just the fear driven, lazy way to do business. But as Chris said in *Never Split The Difference*, "You've got to embrace the hard stuff. That's where the great deals are. And that's what great negotiators do."

Luxury agents also rationalize that they can afford to reduce their fee when the list price is so high. But in what other industry do the top professionals work for *less?*

Flip that rationalization around: if anyone can afford to pay a full fee, it's the high-end client. Those sellers have the money and are used to paying top dollar for what they really want. And when the list price is high, the value of a truly skilled agent is amplified. A great negotiator could mean a difference of hundreds of thousands or millions of dollars in the final sale price. If it takes a full fee agent to get that result, of course they'll pay.

I'm not just making this up. Our coaching clients include plenty of top agents, and we've seen them get full fees even in the top echelons of this business, where everyone says it's impossible. We just had one agent get 6 percent on a $10 million dollar listing. Another sold a $50 million dollar house last year at *7 percent*. It's not impossible. It's just a question of whether you're the Favorite or the Fool, and whether you're fearless enough to stick to your standards.

Excuse #3: There's a special reason for a discount in this case.

There are all kinds of reasons for giving a discount. The client is a friend or family member or a repeat client or a referral or my kid's teacher or my spouse's boss's brother-in-law.

Here's my favorite: *If I represent both sides of the deal, I'll charge 4 percent.*

Whose idea was this? Somehow, this has become a standard practice in the industry, but how does this make sense in any way? When you double end a deal, you still have two jobs to do, and two sets of clients. Where is the logic in reducing your fee by 33 percent?

This same agent, who listed the $50 million dollar property at 7 percent, recently double-ended an $8.6 million dollar deal at 6 percent. During the negotiation, the seller asked the agent to reduce his fee to 4 percent. He simply said, with total deference and respect, "No. We can keep marketing the home to find a buyer who will pay more." The seller happily signed the deal. They just wanted to make sure they weren't leaving any money on the table.

No matter the situation, no matter how you look at it, no matter your motivation, when you choose to discount your fee, you are choosing to work harder to make less.

If you're going to make this decision, make it consciously. The fee you charge ripples out in so many different ways and on so many different levels. Remember, when a discount is the only way to win a client, they're probably a bad client who's going to take up the space of two good, full fee clients.

And while you might think this is an isolated incident, it's not. When you discount this deal, you're also likely to be discounting any future deals or referrals from this client. Plus, you make it easier to justify discounting in other situations. Is that the way you want to run your business?

Like I said before, it's easier to do something 100 percent of the time than 98 percent of the time. Six percent, no exceptions.

COMMISSION CONVERSATIONS WITH
TACTICAL EMPATHY˙

Over many years, I developed what I thought was the perfect commission conversation script. With flawless facts, logic, and reason, it led the prospect to the inevitable conclusion that it would be worth paying 6 percent to get the best possible results. It worked pretty well—better than anything else I'd ever seen.

I threw it in the trash when I met Chris, and have never gone back.

The conversation you need to have is not about facts, logic, and reason. It's about making the other person feel understood. When you apply Tactical Empathy to the commission dialogue, everything changes.

Imagine approaching that conversation with no fear. You're not here to convince anyone. They either want you in their corner or they don't, and you're here to find out.

So, you cross the street and look at the world from their perspective. You reach into their head, read their mind and heart, and get into alignment.

Then, you put the subject out on the table without hesitation. You demonstrate absolute confidence in your very presence. You're not afraid, and they know you will walk. They understand your fee is your fee, and if they want to work with you, that's the number.

Imagine showing up this way every time.

How empowering would that feel? How energizing would that be? What would that inspire inside of you?

How excited would you be to work with people who valued you, respected you, and above all, trusted you?

That's exactly where you'll end up if you apply everything you're learning in this book.

In your mind, this is probably a very big mountain to climb, if not an impossible one. Every part of your ego construct and all of your survival instincts are going to push back hard on this thought. Probably every word in this chapter feels like a suicide mission…but every great experience you have in life is found on the other side of your fears.

Let's break down exactly how to get there. The conversation is always situational, so when you use this framework, always remember to listen closely to the other person, and respond to what's happening in front of you.

1. Prepare your mindset.

Just as with every tough conversation we've talked about in this book, you need to approach it from a place of courage, curiosity, and confidence. Before you enter this situation, take the time to write out what the other person is probably thinking and feeling. Acknowledge your own thoughts and feelings, then let them go. Prepare to focus your full attention on the other person, with the simple goal of discovering what's on their mind.

2. Bring up the issue gently but directly.

For most people, any conversation about money is an awkward one. When you bring it up, use your skills from Chapter 4 to soften the blow.

THE FULL FEE AGENT

At the beginning of the chapter, Regina did this beautifully when she said, "I've got some things we need to talk about that could be deal breakers for you. This is going really well, but I might throw a wrench in the works with this information, so I'd like to put it on the table now. Would you be opposed?"

You don't have to use her words, but you do want to warn the other person that you're about to say something they might not like. Get their permission first.

> There are some reasons why you might not want to work with me. I'd like to tell you about them now in case they're deal breakers for you. Would you be opposed?
>
> Then, say it directly.
>
> I'm a full-service, full fee agent. I charge 6 percent, keep 3.5 percent, and give 2.5 percent to the buyer's agent.

3. Find out what they're thinking and feeling, and make them feel understood.

You want to see through their point of view, and understand why they think that way. It doesn't mean you agree, just that you understand where they're coming from. Once they feel understood, every interaction will become more open and honest.

Start with some labels to find out what results they care about most. Here are some examples:

> You're probably hoping to get top dollar.
>
> You don't want to leave any money on the table.

You would like to pay as little in commission as possible.

Then, use a no-oriented question to establish what matters to them in an agent.

Would it be wrong to assume you want to work with someone who is trustworthy, competent, and a straight shooter? Did I miss anything important?

4. Use calibrated and no-oriented questions to make them think deeply about the role of your fee in their decision.

Most people instinctively want to pay less, but haven't thought through the consequences of that choice. Use a few questions like these to help them engage in that thought process and articulate it to you.

How are you going to factor the commission into your decision-making process?

How are you going to factor the final sale price into your decision-making process?

Would it be crazy to think that at some level, there is a correlation between the fee an agent charges and the results they produce?

What are you willing to give up in return for a lower commission?

What would you need to hear to raise your level of comfort regarding my fee?

Would it be crazy to think that the skill an agent brings to the transaction is more important than the fee they charge?

Would it be crazy to think the fee an agent charges is a direct reflection of their ability to negotiate?

Would it be unreasonable to think that an agent who discounts their fee is giving you a real clue as to their ability to negotiate?

Would it be crazy to think that an agent's ability to negotiate is going to directly impact the final sales price of your home?

Would you be surprised to know that the final sales price of your home can vary 1 to 10 percent or more, up or down, based on your agent's ability to negotiate?

Would it be unreasonable to think the agent who produces a superior result is going to charge more?

Would it be wrong to think what you really want is to net more at the close of escrow?

What are the terms that would make you happy and allow us to go forward right now?

5. Share a story that will help them understand the choice they're facing.

Instead of shoving your track record in their face as evidence of your value, ask permission to share a story that illustrates how an agent can affect the results that matter most to the other person.

This is your opportunity to bend their reality. Change the loss they're focused on: not what am I paying but what could I lose if I choose the wrong agent? Are they willing to risk a $1 million difference in sale price over $20,000 in fees?

You're not trying to convince them, just putting the story out there for them to interpret in their own way. To do that, use a question like this:

Would you be opposed to going through a couple of real life scenarios that illustrate how commission and the final sales price actually impact what you net at the close of escrow?

Are you opposed to hearing why the discount agents can charge so much less and still claim to provide the same results or better?

6. Summarize the choice they're facing and put the ball in their court.

No convincing, no pressure, no fear. Just lay it out for them and let them decide.

What I share with every seller is that in the end, it comes down to who you want in your corner from start to finish. Who do you want guiding you, helping you navigate through the twists and turns of this process? Who do you want negotiating for you, fighting for every last dollar, making sure not to leave any money on the table? Most of all, who do you believe is going to put your interests first at all times, no matter what?

That's the person you hire, regardless of their fee. Do I think I am that person? Yes, but I'm probably a little biased. What's important is, do you think I am that person? If you do, let's work together. If you don't, let's shake hands, wish each other the best, and go our separate ways.

How would you like to proceed?

When you follow this framework, you open the door completely to being the Favorite or the Fool. If you're the Favorite, they're going to hire you there right on the spot. If not, they'll thank you and say they'll get back to you.

7. Address any pushback with proof of life questions.

You might not get a definitive answer immediately. Prospects sometimes push back, even if they do intend to hire you. They might say things like:

Is your fee negotiable?

Other agents are willing to do it for less.

We are really tight on money. We need every penny.

We have done a lot of business with you in the past. Can you give us a break going forward?

I can refer you business. Can you lower your fee?

I thought the going rate was _____?

Wow, that's a lot of money!!

If you sell the home to your own buyer, will you reduce your fee?

This is what we pay.

In the past, we have never paid more than _____ percent. And we have done a lot of business.

If we both buy and sell through you...will you give us a break on commission?

Do you offer a friends and family discount?

You are a small independent. Can't you be flexible?

(Developers) If we give you the listing on the back end, will you work for less on the purchase?

Instead of giving in or explaining why you can't, use a proof of life question to find out if they're serious about working with you. For example:

Why would you do business with me?

Why would you pay me 6 percent?

Why would you pay me more?

With all the other agents who are willing to work for less, why would you pay my full fee?

It seems like you are not opposed to the idea of working together...we just have to come to terms regarding commission.

Are you opposed to the idea of working with me, even though my fee is higher?

It sounds like you are not convinced you need to hire me in order to sell your home for top dollar.

It sounds like you have another agent in mind who charges less.

It sounds like someone else may be a better choice for you.

Are you totally and completely against the idea of working with me because my fee is higher?

If they can articulate why they want to do business with you, you're the Favorite, and they'll agree to your fee. If not, you're the Fool, and it's time to send them away in a limo.

Occasionally, you might even get pushback after a client hires you. For example, one of our coaching clients recently double-ended a $70 million listing. After the deal was done, the seller came back and asked for a 1 percent reduction in fee.

The agent was stunned. She knew she had done a great job, and sold the house at top dollar.

She called the seller and said, "I'm really sorry. I must have done a horrible job for you."

The seller replied, "No, you did an incredible job!"

So, the agent said, "Then I'm confused...it seems like I'm being punished."

That was all it took to get the seller to backtrack and happily accept the full fee.

THE FEE OR THE FEELING

When it comes to commission, what is truly most important to a seller? Is it the fee you charge, or the feeling you give them in terms of how they are going to be taken care of in the transaction?

Once again, you must take your own feelings out of the equation. Most agents approach the commission discussion full of fear. If you do that, you'll try to convince the seller that you're the best person for the job, relying on facts, logic, and reason to persuade them of your value. You'll believe you need to tell them all the wonderful things you're going to do for them to justify why they should hire you.

This path leads you into the trap of making yourself a commodity. The more you share and explain, the less valuable you become in the eyes of the potential client you are speaking with. Remember: when you're explaining, you're losing.

Instead, your new approach is to turn the commission discussion into a conversation about trust. Rather than defending your fee, you're focusing on who the seller really wants to represent them. We broke that process down into steps in the last section. Here's how it sounds all together.

Seller: Why should I pay you more?

Agent: It's probably confusing that different agents charge different fees.

Seller: Yes, it is confusing.

Agent: Would it be wrong to assume that what you really want is to make sure you're not overpaying, and you're not leaving any money on the table?

Seller: That's right.

Agent: When it comes to selecting an agent to represent you in the sale of your home, I share this guidance with every potential seller...would you be opposed if I share it with you?

Seller: Please do.

Agent: When it comes to selecting your agent, choose the one who gives you the highest level of confidence in achieving the best outcome possible. Who you believe will best prepare and position you for success... Who you believe will best help you navigate through the selling process from start to finish...Who you believe will best protect your interests at all times. That is the person you want to hire, regardless of their fee.

Just like that, you've moved this dialogue from a number to a feeling.

If you're the Favorite, the door is wide open for them to choose you in that moment. More than anything else, the commission discussion revolves around whether you're the Favorite or the Fool...and that comes down to a feeling of trust.

This Is Your Moment of Truth

As Steven Ross said, "Paying my full fee is the litmus test for having a great client."

Your commission is the cornerstone of your business. When you set your standard at 6 percent and stick to it fearlessly, everything else you've learned in this book must follow. It's impossible to uphold that standard successfully unless you practice everything else you've learned about Tactical Empathy. The 6 percent fee forces you to commit to that practice 100 percent.

You may have other standards you want to uphold in your business. For example, Regina always has her clients stage their homes and price to sell quickly. She also doesn't work Saturdays or answer the phone after 6 p.m. That's what it takes to run her business and life the way she wants, and it's nonnegotiable.

But, she doesn't have to have a tough conversation about each of those things. If she can get past the commission issue with a prospect, she knows they'll accept those things. If she can't, it doesn't matter.

The same is true for you. Set standards for how you work so that your business actually serves you and creates the life you want. Lay them out up front, just as Regina did. Just like your commission, those are reasons someone might not want to work with you.

But by far, the commission is the most important of all the standards. If a prospect agrees to that, they'll agree to it all.

That's why this whole chapter has focused exclusively on this one issue. Becoming a full-service, full fee agent is the culmination of everything you've learned in this book. It requires you to make the switch from transactions to relationships, from explaining your value to building trust, and from convincing to making people feel understood.

KEY TAKEAWAYS

→ Everything you've learned so far comes together in the most important discussion you'll have with any client: the commission conversation.

→ If you're the Favorite, they'll agree to your fee. If you're not, it doesn't matter what your fee is—they probably won't hire you anyway.

→ There are all kinds of excuses for giving discounts, but none of them hold water. You and your clients are both better off if you stick to the standard of 6 percent, no exceptions.

→ Typical scripts for this conversation use facts, logic, and reason to try to convince the prospect of your worth. Throw them in the trash. Instead, use what you've learned about Tactical Empathy to lay out the issue and guide their decision.

→ This is your moment of truth, where you either challenge yourself to become a full-service, full fee agent with a business built on trust...or you get stuck in the status quo.

CONCLUSION

It's time to get your humanity—
and your life—back.

Congratulate yourself! You've made it all the way to the end of this book, which means you were open-minded enough and value yourself enough to consider a new way of doing things. It probably seemed insane at first. Certainly, most of the things you've learned go completely against what agents typically do, and there are plenty of people who would tell you you're crazy to try this.

Hopefully, you've been paying close enough attention to realize by now that while it may be scary to change, it's the sanest decision you will ever make. To quote Frank Zappa, "Without deviation from the norm, progress is not possible."

Before, you were turning yourself into a commodity. You spent all your time chasing clients, convincing them to do what you want, and pushing everyone to close the deal. Chase, convince, close, over and over in a never-ending cycle of fear, attachment, hope, and disappointment.

In your eagerness for more clients, more revenue, more prestige, more everything...you made yourself a slave to the transaction.

It's time to get your humanity—and your life—back.

It starts with recognizing how people actually think and make decisions. We're not machines who see the world without bias and weigh all the pros and cons mathematically. We're human beings with feelings and brains that have evolved to keep us alive, not to be unbiased. If there's one thing about human nature you always remember, let it be this: you can't overcome emotion with fact, logic, and reason.

Because of that, and because there's no such thing as an open mind, you've completely transformed the way you approach prospects. There is no convincing anyone to hire you—their minds are already made up. All you have to do is find out whether you're the Favorite or the Fool. When you use Tactical Empathy to make them feel understood, they'll reveal the answer to you. Instead of spending days on a listing appointment, you figure out within half an hour whether you really have a shot. If not, you happily walk away and save your time for the people who *want* to work with you.

Now, in every client relationship, you have a new focus: building trust. Gone are the days of explaining your value and giving away your time, effort, and money to win people over. You know now that the indirect route is faster. By building trust, you pave the way for every future interaction to be easier, more productive, and more joyful. All you have to do is let go of your own feelings and desires, then focus your complete attention on the other person. It's that simple.

You're not scared of tough conversations anymore, either. You used to avoid or sugarcoat them, but that just undermined your clients' trust in you. Now, you call out the negatives and break bad news as soon as possible, gently and with confidence. You've learned how to brace them for it and use Accusations Audits to make them feel understood. You've also used Accusations Audits to examine your own feelings and set them aside, so you can focus on the other person.

You've also stopped taking on responsibility for things that are outside your control. Before, you felt like it was your job to steer every choice and solve every problem. Now, you recognize that in the end, only the client can decide anything. Your job is just to be the trusted advisor who provides all the information they need to make informed, empowered choices. Your stress, angst, and frustration don't help—they just get in the way. So, you let it go and focus on guiding the client's decisions, not owning them.

To do that effectively, you've learned to start with no instead of pushing for yes. People hate to say yes—it makes them feel vulnerable and puts them on guard. Saying no, on the other hand, protects them and preserves their autonomy. After they say no, they're more open to hearing what you have to say. So, to guide your client, you begin with no-oriented questions. Then, you use calibrated (how and what) questions to help them think through tough issues and share what they truly want and don't want.

You've learned to use these Tactical Empathy techniques all the time, from the beginning of the relationship to the end—especially the end. The last impression is the lasting impression, and people who walk away feeling good about you are more likely to come back and refer other people to you. That's exactly what you need to build a sustainable business. So, you follow the Oprah Rule: send everyone away in a limo, no matter what.

All of this comes together in one single moment of truth: the commission conversation. It's the most important conversation you have with your clients, and the one that agents dread the most...but not you, because now you're a full-service, full fee agent. Your standard is 6 percent, and you stick to it 100 percent of the time. It's not because you're greedy. It's because charging 6 percent forces you to do everything else you've learned in this book. It challenges you to be the best agent you can be every day, and it rewards you with a business that's a joy instead of a drain on your life.

This book is not about following a series of steps to get what you want. It's about showing up as a human being who's here to serve other human beings, with no other agenda. You don't have to be a real estate machine who sacrifices their personal life and happiness to do business. You can be authentic and real, and *that's* the way to do more business in way less time, with way less stress. Instead of just surviving, you can start living your highest and best.

Remember, how you do business is more important than how much business you do. When you focus on the *how*, the score will take care of itself.

START BY LETTING GO

I've said it over and over in this book, and I'll say it again: your feelings and desires have no place here. They are getting in your way. Start by letting them go.

You've been conditioned your whole life to believe that if you want something good to happen, you have to make it happen. You have to convince people to follow you and fight against everything that blocks your path. It's a constant battle between you and the universe, and you must get your way.

As Michael Singer put it in his book, *The Surrender Experiment*:

The battle between individual will and the reality of life unfolding around us ends up consuming our lives. When we win the battle, we are happy and relaxed; when we don't, we're disturbed and stressed. Since most of us only feel good when things are going our way, we are constantly attempting to control everything in our lives.

That is not a peaceful existence. You spend all your time fighting to get what you think you need to be happy, but it's *the fight itself* that's killing your happiness.

With this book, you've learned how to stop fighting.

You're not here to make something happen. Instead, you show up, giving your highest and best to *what is* happening. How many times have you read those words already? If you take them to heart, it will take all the stress and struggle out of your work. Your business will transform from something that drains your life force to something that brings you joy and peace.

None of this is just about business either. Humans are humans, and our minds work the same in business and in our personal lives. Every single thing you've learned can apply just as well to your spouse, your kids, your parents, or your friends as it does to your clients. Tactical Empathy can transform all your relationships, if you let it.

THREE THINGS TO MASTER

Tactical Empathy is a learned skill, and to start using it in your business, your habits have to change. If you're like most of the agents we coach, you're used to winging your client conversations and getting by on personality. That's not going to cut it anymore.

Replacing old habits with new ones takes deliberate practice. If you let yourself wing it, you'll default to your old ways and never make progress.

We've hit you with a lot of new skills in this book, and we don't expect you to master them all at once. These are the three you need to start with. The conversation hasn't really begun until these three things happen.

1. Prepare.

Get in the habit of taking time each day to anticipate upcoming conversations and write down what the other person will likely be thinking and feeling. Then, write down what you're thinking and feeling, including all your hopes and fears about the outcome of the conversation... and let them go. They don't matter, and they will only get in your way.

Whatever the interaction is—talking to a prospect, hosting an open house, writing an offer—prepare your mind to focus on the other person.

2. Read the situation.

Your old habit was to show up ready to push your agenda. Instead, you need to show up ready to read the other person. Focus exclusively on them and pay attention to the details—not just what they're saying but also their body language, tone of voice, and what they're *not* saying. Preparation makes this easier because it helps you know what to look for, just as reading scouting reports helped me read the situation on the field when I was in the NFL.

3. Make them feel understood.

Your only goal is to get them to say "that's right." Use mirrors and labels to elicit more information and confirm your understanding until you sense that emotional click, when you get in alignment with them. That's how you know you've successfully crossed to their side of the street and seen the world from their perspective.

IT'S HARD...UNTIL IT'S NOT

I have a coaching client who is supposed to do expired listing calls every day, as part of his prospecting plan. He never does it, and every time we talk about it, he dreads it more and more.

Every day you don't do something, it gets harder. But when you let go of your excuses and just do it, it keeps getting easier.

I'll give you an extreme example from my personal life. A while back, I got a Peloton and pledged to ride it every single day. I started at five or ten miles a day and worked my way up to sixty.

Then, I thought: what if I rode one hundred miles a day for one hundred days?

It knew it would be hard at first. I had only ridden one hundred miles twice, once back in my twenties, and once on the Peloton a few months prior. But, I wanted to know how riding one hundred miles would feel after I had done it one hundred times.

Instead of approaching it with unhelpful thoughts and feelings about what I expected (*This is going to be so hard...I'm not sure I have the energy for this today...I'm already sore from yesterday...blah, blah, blah*), I got on the bike each day with an attitude of surrender.

I had made the commitment. I had no choice but to be there, on that bike, riding one hundred miles. I wasn't there to make something happen, but to discover what would happen. How would it feel to ride one hundred miles today?

Day one? Not so bad. Day two? Not so bad. Day three? Same thing.

By the time I had done it ten times, it was easy. There was no question I could do it.

That's what I'm asking you to do with Tactical Empathy. Commit to the decision to do it, and surrender to that commitment. Just do it —feel the fear, let it go, and do it anyway. There's a big difference between wondering if you can do it and working to get better. The first is a never-ending trap. The second lets you feed off the progress.

Forming new habits means building new neural pathways and using them over and over. The more you use them, the stronger they get, and the more your old pathways atrophy. When the new ones are stronger than the old ones, you have a new habit.

To make this happen, you've got to put in the reps.

Find low-stakes situations where you can practice these skills without taking big risks. Role play with your colleagues. Apply them in your personal life. At an open house, pick one label and use it on everyone who comes in, and practice reading whether they're a serious buyer or not.

When I first started practicing Tactical Empathy, I had to really think about it every time, and it felt unnatural. I just kept at it, and the awkwardness dissipated. Now, my brain is totally rewired, and it's almost effortless.

But it doesn't take years to get comfortable with this. Most of the time, it only takes a few reps to tip the balance from awkward and painful to exciting and fun.

For example, Chris has a technique based on Tactical Empathy for getting free upgrades at hotels. When he traveled for the first time after the COVID shutdown, he was reluctant to use it, even though he knew it was effective.

Unhelpful thoughts and feelings were running through his mind: *I don't have the energy for this...I'm out of practice...It probably won't work anyway.*

But he surrendered to his commitment to Tactical Empathy and did it anyway. It's just three simple steps:

1. "I'm getting ready to ruin your whole day." Brace the concierge for bad news.
2. "I know I'm about to sound like a self-centered, demanding

traveler who is so self-involved that they want something for nothing." Do a quick Accusations Audit.

3. "How much trouble will you get in if you give me a free upgrade to a suite?" Use a calibrated question to make them think about your request from a fresh perspective. The answer is usually none, which makes them happy to do it.

It worked. In fact, it worked at eight out of the nine hotels he stayed in on that trip, and it only failed in a hotel where all the rooms were suites anyway. After the fourth time, he no longer felt even the slightest internal resistance to doing it.

Give yourself at least four tries. By the fourth rep, it will feel noticeably easier than the first time. That's enough motivation to keep you going to the tenth rep, and the twentieth, and the hundredth, until you've lost count and it's just how you do business.

LET YOURSELF TRANSFORM

Most agents have figured out how to do business. They just haven't figured out how to do business *and* have a life.

When my coaching clients start practicing Tactical Empathy and experiencing the results, they start asking a whole new set of questions. *I have all this time...what do I do? Can I really just relax and watch Netflix? Should I get a hobby? Get a dog? Start dating again?*

If you're one of the many, *many* real estate agents who has let your business take over your entire life, this will be you. It might sound funny when you read it, but this is serious stuff. These people are finally confronting the question: If I'm not just my business, who am I? Why am I here? What am I doing with my life?

That's how deep this really goes.

Tactical Empathy is not just another way to marginally improve your business results and go on your merry way. It is transformational. It changes everything: your relationships, your business, and your entire life.

We challenge you to *let it change you.*

Just like the clients who come to me for coaching, you picked up this book because you know you can do better. You know deep down that you're not a commodity; you're more than your production, and your clients are more than a paycheck.

You're a human being, here to serve other human beings.

For Further Negotiation Training Please Visit The Black Swan Group at www.blackswanltd.com.

ACKNOWLEDGMENTS

FROM STEVE SHULL

As a former professional football player, every year I look forward to the NFL Hall of Fame induction ceremonies. I love listening to the speeches given by each new gold jacket recipient, and what I love most is how each new Hall of Fame member says thank you to all the people in their lives that have made this accomplishment possible. Unfortunately, I am never going into the NFL Hall of Fame. However, in writing this book with my coauthor Chris Voss, I am now getting my chance to say thank you and acknowledge all the people who have influenced me greatly along my life journey.

First, I want to start with Chris Voss. As I share in the following pages, reading Chris's book *Never Split The Difference* was a real game changer for me. The moment I read the book, I knew I had to reach out to Chris, and the book you are about to read is the byproduct of all the work we have done together over the past five years. I thank you, Chris, and I know all my clients thank you as well.

And speaking of clients, I want to make a huge shout out to a very select group of coaching clients who have supported me and believed in me and worked with me for a very long time. All my clients are valuable and important to me, however this group has a very special place in my heart and mind: Vickey England, Terri and David Elston, Elaine Stucy (who wrote the forward), Stephanie Younger, Sally Forster Jones, Linda May, Jeffrey and Nadia Saad, Regina Vannicola, Mark Javonovich and Scott Hustis, and Dana Green and Santiago Arana. You are my Hall of Fame clients, and it has been the greatest privilege to work with each of you.

Another group of special people I want to thank include my football coaches: Pal Allison (high school); Lou Tepper, Wally Ake, and Jim Root (college); and Steve Crosby, Bill Arnsbarger, and Don Shula (professional). All of these men believed in me and taught me lessons I use every day in my coaching practice and life.

The following individuals have also been important teachers and mentors in my life, directly and indirectly: Pete Certo, David Allen, Fred Wilson, Betty Graham, Larry Kendall, Robert Reffkin, Ryan Holiday, Patrick Sweeny, and Michael Singer. Your wisdom is greatly appreciated.

And since I am not sure when I will get this chance again, I would like to make a heartfelt mention of my early childhood heroes: Johnny Callison, Wilt Chamberlain, Arnold Palmer, and Muhammad Ali. All of you stoked my imagination in a very significant way.

Next is my best friend in life, Jamie Leder: You have always been by my side, no matter what. I love you, man.

To Madison Fitzpatrick: I hope you know this book wouldn't have gotten written without you. THANK YOU!!

To Danielle Lazier and Sean McGlynn: thank you for being the pioneers and early adopters of this new methodology.

To my Dad: I was probably way too tough on you in life, but I always realized you were my biggest cheerleader.

To my mom: thank you for always reminding me and challenging me to be better.

To my brother and sister: The journey is not over yet. Let's all stay open to what's next.

To my incredible daughters, Sophia and Sasha: Talk about keeping a man honest! You are my heartbeat and my touchstone. I love you both so dearly, and hopefully you know you are a big part of this book.

Finally, to the love of my life, my wife Katerina: Without your never-ending support and encouragement (code for your foot up my ass), none of what I do is possible. You are my coach, and I love you for it!

FROM CHRIS VOSS

This book would not have been possible without Brandon Voss and the entire Black Swan Group team. Brandon met Steve and told me, "You have to talk with this guy. We should work with him." He was right. Then, the entire Black Swan Group team, Vannessa Bernal in particular, kicked into gear and supported all our efforts. If you want to go fast, go alone. If you want to go far, go as a team. Thank you, Team Black Swan!

ABOUT THE AUTHORS

STEVE SHULL is a former linebacker for the Miami Dolphins. When an injury forced him to change his game—literally—he pivoted into finance, then real estate, and found his calling when he started coaching other agents. Twenty-three years later, he read a book by Chris Voss, tossed out his playbook, and redesigned the whole program from scratch.

CHRIS VOSS served as the lead international kidnapping negotiator for the FBI. His business negotiation book *Never Split the Difference* has sold millions of copies around the world. After twenty-four years with the Bureau, he founded The Black Swan Group to help realtors, companies, and individuals take their negotiation skills to the next level.

Printed in Great Britain
by Amazon